C000057164

Skeletons in Messiah's Cupboard

Overcoming your genetic baggage

Gethin Russell-Jones

Scripture Union

Scripture Union, 207–209 Queensway, Bletchley, MK2 2EB, England.

Email: info@scriptureunion.org.uk
Internet: http://www.scriptureunion.org.uk

© Copyright Gethin Russell-Jones 2001

First published 2001
ISBN 1 85999464 4

All rights reserved. No part of this publication may be reproduced, stored in a retrieval system, or transmitted, in any form or by any means, electronic, mechanical, photocopying, recording or otherwise, without the prior permission of Scripture Union.

The right of Gethin Russell-Jones to be identified as author of this work has been asserted by him in accordance with the Copyright, Designs and Patents Act 1988.

Scripture taken from: THE HOLY BIBLE, NEW INTERNATIONAL VERSION. Copyright © 1973, 1978, 1984 by International Bible Society. Anglicisation copyright © 1979, 1984, 1989. Used by permission of Hodder and Stoughton Limited. *The Contemporary English Version*, ©1997 British and Foreign Bible Society. *THE MESSAGE*. Copyright © by Eugene H Peterson, 1993, 1994, 1995. Used by permission of NavPress Publishing Group.

British Library Cataloguing-in-Publication Data
A catalogue record for this book is available from the British Library.

Cover design by ie Design.
Printed and bound in Great Britain by Stanley L Hunt (Printers) Ltd, Rushden, Northamptonshire.

To Anna, Bronwen, Thomas and Adam — my bundle of life.

The characters portrayed in this book are based on real people, but in all instances the names have been changed. In several instances some disguise has been given to a few facts which may have enabled identification. And in some instances the characters described are a composite creation based on more than one person. There is no intention to cause any harm or damage to any individuals or to their reputations; rather, care has been taken to protect the identity of the characters while at the same time portraying real-life situations.

Contents

About Gethin Russell-Jones, author of *Skeletons in Messiah's Cupboard*

Gethin's career has not always been poetic. Working in a pasta restaurant he describes as 'the hardest work I've ever done.' Somewhere along the road he has trained as a barrister, sold tele sales ads and worked on a radio station. But foundational to his writing is the time he spent pastoring two Baptist churches, which has drawn out of him an impulse to describe in words the gracious activity of God in the lives of broken people.

'Families can be wonderful and dreadful,' says Gethin, 'frequently at the same time! For many, the family is place of safety, love and understanding. For others it's a bay of dangerous currents, and hidden, dangerous wreckage. But the family is more than its present expression. Through my parents, I am connected to vast generations of ancestors, whilst my children fuse me to the future. I am part of a wonderful gallery of faith, folly and wisdom, a family where humanity is celebrated in all its beauty and failure. This was also Jesus' experience. Matthew's first chapter is a celebration of God's purposes worked out in Jesus' strange, sometimes dysfunctional, family tree. Just like the rest of us.'

Yes, Gethin was born in Wales. And, yes, he really does live now in Milton Keynes, working in journalism and public relations. He's married to Clare and they have four children.

They read it first, and they said...

'As a Christian counsellor I found this book totally absorbing, refreshingly different and extremely thought-provoking. A book I simply could not put down!'
Jennifer Rees Larcombe,
counsellor, agony aunt, author

'An important resource for all those exploring and engaging with challenges facing Christian discipleship today.'
Inderjit Bhogal,
President of UK Methodists

'I have never considered Jesus's ancestors in this light before, and what a motley crew they turned out to be! Anyone feeling held back or haunted by their families and their past should definitely read this book. A wonderful read – I couldn't put it down!' Frances, working mum

'Through this book we appreciate afresh the very human nature of Jesus ... and how the Bible is full of struggling people "just like us". Through a lively mix of biblical accounts and up-to-date real-life stories, *Skeletons in Messiah's Cupboard* draws us closer to the Christ who not only understands but brings hope – whatever our background, upbringing or current circumstances.'
Liz Trundle, Editor, Woman Alive

'These harrowing situations are reality for so many people and I have not come across a Christian book like this which faces them head-on, tells the outcome in real-life circumstances and presents not only the "human" side of Jesus, but also shows him as the one who can change life around. A big difference between this book and others that present Jesus as the answer is that this one shows that the struggles still continue, post-conversion, and it does not provide pat, glib answers.' Eleanor, fifty-something part-time PA, wife and mother

'The message of this book is so simple, but its power lies in its applicability to just about every human on this planet – for everyone who has ever felt wounded, let down, screwed up in their search for security and belonging in human relationships. We don't have to be bound by past hurts, but in the power of Christ's love can move forward into new life as a member of God's family, secure in his perfect, unconditional love for his children. A truly encouraging and uplifting read! Lucy, twenty-something charity worker

intro

In 1859, a young woman took a walk along the river Cothi in the idyllic county of Carmarthenshire, South Wales. A Sunday afternoon, and this youthful maid Mary was enjoying a brief interlude before preparation started for the evening meal. She was in the service of Timothy Richard, a gentleman missionary to China, who had pioneered Christian activity in the exotic sub-continent. As she turned a bend on the river bank, she heard the sound of singing. A little nearer and she caught a glimpse of people ahead of her. Within a few hundred yards the bank was **a gala of people**, thousands of them. Three were actually in the water. The Welsh hymn that was being sung was familiar to her:

> Pan oeddwn I mewn carchar tywyll du
> Rhoest I'm oleuni, rhoest I'm oleuni,
> Rhoest I'm oleuni nefol.
> Haleliwia, haleliwia, haleliwia, amen.
>
> When I was in the darkest dungeon deep,
> You gave me light, You gave me light,
> You gave me light from heaven.
> Hallelujah, hallelujah, hallelujah, amen.

This was the year of revival. William Williams and Ann Griffiths were penning their hymns. Hundreds of thousands in this small country developed **enormous appetites for Jesus Christ**. Not only in Wales, but in Scotland, Northern Ireland and America. And my great-grandmother Mary was there, witnessing and part of that revival, that moment in history.

I know very little about her. In fact nothing, other than these few fragments. But they mean more to me than inherited wealth. In my more fanciful moments, I feel I'm carrying that moment, her moment, around in my body, `swimming in my genes`. I've told it to my children and if they have any, no doubt they will tell theirs. Sometimes the cry of the past is benign...

But not always.

I know someone whose years of childhood and adolescence were marked by middle-class comforts: top boarding school, foreign travel, full-time nanny during the holidays. But her memories are skewered by one painful event. During one holiday, aged about twelve, she was woken by the sound of a sickening thud. The sort of noise generated by an unprotected head colliding with concrete. Running to the nearest window, she saw her father lying prostrate on the patio, her mother standing over him. 'Daddy, daddy,' she wailed. He lived, severe bruising to his body... but **the internal breakage** was incalculable. A suicide attempt that had gone wrong. Seldom referred to now, but this incident marked an emotional death in the family.

I know another someone who comes from a very large family. She is one of eleven children, living only a matter of a few miles from her family home. She shares residency of this small town with eight of her siblings. Living within a few streets of each other, they visit the same post office, the same supermarket, shops. But **they never meet**. In fact this woman hasn't spoken to either her parents or siblings for over twenty years. They might as well live on remote islands. Some distant and bitter feud has poisoned their relationships. As far as she's concerned, she doesn't care whether she speaks to them again before her death.

I know another someone who grew up in the UK but now lives in Perth, Australia. Her parents still live in England, as do her brother and sister. Neither she nor her husband enjoy particularly well-paid occupations but she made a decision about priorities some years ago. She decided that she would visit her parents five times a year, and pay for them to visit her once a year. This imposes a financial strain, sustained only by living in the red. She thinks **it's worth it.**

So there are families that work and many that don't...

chapter 1: dirty laundry

> A record of the genealogy of Jesus Christ the son of David, the son of Abraham: Abraham was the father of Isaac, Isaac the father of Jacob, Jacob the father of Judah and his brothers, Judah the father of Perez and Zerah, whose mother was Tamar... **Matthew 1:1-3**

Jesus came from a dysfunctional family. True? Well, his human ancestry was as compromised and fractured as any one else's. Worse, if anything. **Prostitution, adultery, incest, alienation.** Not to mention **teenage pregnancy.** Hardly reasons to celebrate, but not unusual. As old as time and the human family, these disturbing social manifestations still have power to create shame, or embarrassment. Or, to put it another way, how would you feel if you discovered that these five characteristics were in your family? Should you stumble upon these distressing facts in your family tree, your inclination would be towards privacy. Again, imagine that a well-known journalist captures your most intimate data and publicises it in the national media, or over the Internet. You'd feel exposed, shamed, angry that your personal life had been trawled over, dragged through the public gutter.

This is what routinely happens to Britain's royal family. When Diana, Princess of Wales, died tragically in 1997, it re-awakened rumours of power rifts in the Queen's household, along with gutter fables concerning former lovers.

This is what happened to Jesus. Not for him a Mercedes careering fatally into a Parisian tunnel or an exposé of some salacious detail. Worse. His family's **dirty laundry** has been hung out to dry for two thousand years, appearing in the world's best selling book, probably in your living room.

Matthew Chapter 1 isn't the most sizzling part of the Bible. It yields very few sermons, simply serving to hurry the reader on to archangels, wise men from the east and, of course, the donkey. It's a family tree. There are some whose appetites are whetted by complex genealogies. But not many. Ancestor tracing has become a popular pastime for some, although the majority know more about their pet's pedigree than their great grandparents' place of birth.

The research is time-consuming, hard work, and the finishing line is a mass of loose ends. Curiosity and confusion can easily bring family tree houses crashing down. For some, however, dogged perseverance in the face of changed names, false names and nicknames, brings the answers they've been looking for all their lives.

There's nothing strange about Matthew including Jesus' family tree. Storytellers do it now, and the human race has always done it. But his intention is peculiar. Matthew's account of Jesus' life, death and resurrection serves several purposes. He wants to:

- portray the Jewishness of Jesus...

- demonstrate that Jesus fulfilled Old Testament prophecy...

- identify Jesus as God's unique messenger, deserving of greater attention than other religious figures.

Yet none of this really explains Matthew's outrageous first chapter. At the time when this was written, it's incontrovertible that women were hardly ever mentioned in Jewish genealogies, except when there were significant gaps in the male line, and even then they had to be especially holy or virtuous.

So why, Matthew? Why mention five women in the family tree of Jesus whose infamous stories arouse great controversy and even shame? What's the point of celebrating God's new and perfect messenger while associating him with twisted deeds and compromised people?

There is no straightforward answer. Here are four possibilities:

- Just by having the women there, we are introduced to Jesus' concern for sinners and non-Jews.

- The presence of the women shows how God can use unlikely people to do his work.

- Perhaps the women are all like Mary in some ways, and so introduce her story.

Maybe Matthew is pre-empting attacks on Jesus by arguing that good King David also came from a broken home.

No one knows. Their presence on the page today is still scandalous and Matthew must have realised this. In this book we shall meet Matthew's five women, exploring dark themes:

- sleeping with your father-in-law and having his babies: Tamar's story.

- working as a hooker in a city destroyed by God, and having your life saved by him: Rahab's story.

- outsider trading: Ruth the wanderer becomes part of the family.

Skeletons: the dark stories of Matthew's five women.

- what a great fall: why all the king's men couldn't put Bathsheeba together again.

- teenage pregnancy: Mary is found with child, outside the law of the land.

History doesn't record how Jesus responded to his identifying features. There was no Internet and no ancestry industry, and no systematic dispersion of the generations. You could argue along these lines...

But you'd be wrong. During the reign of Caesar Augustus, as Luke puts it, there was **the mother of all genealogical headaches.** Every male had to return to his place of birth. Joseph, Mary and the foetus Jesus journeyed from the northern town of Galilee to the soft underbelly of Judea's South East, namely Bethlehem. Joseph, if he didn't already know it, became acquainted with his family's absurdities. <u>Jesus may have been the lamb of God but he came from a line of black sheep.</u>

There are black sheep in your family. It could be you. Likely as not, you haven't spoken to them for a long time. Maybe you've been in the relational wilderness for years, abandoned by the judgement of others. They didn't understand, they never do. Or so you say.

Like this young man, Anthony. He visited a counsellor a few years ago, because... Because God knows why. Young accountant, prospects, going somewhere. But he was plagued by an appalling relationship with his father. Not abuse in the accepted use of the term, something more subtle. More middle-class. Years of career absence, frowning, vacillation, had left its marks on Anthony. **Haunted** by a memory of sorts. Might have been a dream, but he couldn't be sure. He was lying in a bed and felt very young. Five or six. Dark, quiet, eerily still. It was an old-fashioned kind of bed, wrought iron,

Anthony's skeleton – haunted by a memory of his father.

heavy blankets, cold air. In the doorway, in front of the closed door, stood a man. His father. Wearing a blank expression, his dad stared at him, saying nothing.

Anthony still sees him, not every night, but it's an inner vision he returns to regularly. Not a happy memory, but one spiked with feelings of fear and dread. Why? It's a disjointed, out-of-socket picture with no before or after. It leads nowhere, but still he feels anxious, twenty-seven years later.

Fearful of authority figures, Anthony is plagued in his relationships, especially at work. Although successful in his professional qualifications, he feels pulled by two contradictory reactions: fear — he conforms to the wishes of those whom he perceives to be powerful personalities; and rebellion — he actively seeks to undermine these people through his work and private attitudes.

He finds trust difficult. His counsellor defines his problem. Critical silence. Taking him back to that strange and dreamful memory, he identifies this as the key issue.

Janice has a family of her own now, but grew up as a single child:

'I have no brothers and sisters and both my parents died several years ago. Having my own children and grandchildren means I have someone of my own.

'I always wanted siblings. When I was first born my parents shared their house with my father's brother and his family. So when I came home from the nursing home, there was a two-year-old in the house and within six months of my birth another baby was born to my uncle and aunt. We all lived together until I was four, when my uncle died and my aunt took my cousins to America. I lost touch with them, apart from the odd letter/parcel from people I had absolutely no memory of, but we got back together once we were in our twenties and the younger of my two cousins, the one nearer to my age, is my best friend and confidant. We visit as often as we can and each time we part it gets harder to say goodbye. I always felt I should have had an older brother but could never understand why I felt like that. I imagine, now that I can assess it, that I have some vague memory of that cousin but that the trauma of losing him blocked it out.'

Lara's story resounds with family riches:

'Coming from a large extended East London family, I value the support of the family. The loyalty — the feeling of all being in it together (whatever 'it' may be). I have never felt alone or lonely. **I have always felt loved.** I can't imagine what it must be like to be unloved. I didn't become a Christian until my late forties. I would have liked to have been a Christian much earlier so that I could have given my children a Christian upbringing. I regret that very much, but I couldn't have loved them any more.'

'I have always felt loved.' For some this is the

most

    natural

        thing

            in the world.

The words remind others of the

        howling

    emptiness

within.

Like it or loathe it, we are all part of something called family. There are still people who have two parents who live together, even sleep in the same bed. May have siblings.

But the picture is beginning to seem a little dated.

Not so long ago I visited a small village. The usual stuff: thatched cottages, chestnut trees, Landrovers, dogs. Lots of dogs. I passed a church, a small Victorian chapel, of the non-Conformist variety. Glancing at the neat graveyard, daffodils, I was nearly past it when I noticed the board. The Notice Board. You know, that worthy piece of three by three which adorns the outside of most churches. With words such as:

WISE MEN SOUGHT JESUS — THEY STILL DO

or

CARPENTER FROM NAZARETH SEEKS JOINERS

or a more contemporary version

THE MILLENNIUM BELONGS TO JESUS.
WORSHIP HIM HERE. NOW.

By the way, the last statement is a contractual breach. Ecclesiastical misrepresentation, a puff. If you've ever seen this line outside a church, as likely as not, **the doors are closed**. You can't get in. You can't worship him here now, at least not in the way intended by the slogan. Worshipping Jesus on a damp pavement can be done, but it doesn't need a fanfare of hyperbole to achieve it.

However. Back to that poster in the village churchyard. You know the sort of thing. Faded, two-colour, it had probably hung there for years. COME TO CHURCH THIS SUNDAY reads the gripping headline. Standing erect underneath the sans-serif type face are five individuals. Actually, four are standing and one in a pram. A mummy, a daddy, Janet, John and Jocasta. Dad is wearing a mackintosh, tightly buttoned, tie, side parting and, incongruously, a rakish grin. Mum is holding the pram, dressed dowdily, gazing adoringly at the young Jocasta. Jocasta looks quizzical. Yes, quizzical, even though she's only six months old. Janet is wearing a knee-length coat, and looks as though she'd rather be anywhere else in the world. John is a rebel. Sure, he's clad in knee-length shorts and a mandatory grey v-neck pullover. But, he is without a tie. **A rebel without a tie.** Look at his face and you'll see a look of mild pain. White, tidily dishevelled (an obvious middle-class trait) and cheesy. Very white and very cheesy.

Such was the visual impact that I stopped, gasped gently and felt rather faint. It was like seeing an old advert from the 1960s, profiling **a product that no longer exists.** Generations of dentures, furniture restorers, hair cream and suppositories have long since disappeared, leaving only their promotional plans in some archive or another. A few of them produced TV ads, the kind laughed at in 'Adverts from Hell' or suchlike TV blunders sorts of programmes. That's where this poster belonged. It should have been consigned to a museum of holy horrors, filed deep in a subterranean crypt. But no, here it was in broad daylight, belching an image as contemporary as Muffin the Mule.

I stood, appalled at this cheeseboard of Christianity. I should have torn the poster down and sent it to the Keeper of Antiquities at the British Museum.

It's hard to define what *family* means these days, but it rarely looks like that poster. Some modern models of family:

■ married man and woman, legally bound together for life, with children;

■ lone parent with child/children;

■ man and woman, unmarried, cohabiting;

■ married man and woman without children;

■ unmarried man and woman with children;

- two people of the same sex, cohabiting, enjoying sexual relations;

- two people of the same sex, in a sexual relationship, parenting children;

- a group of people, cohabiting, not in sexual relationships with each other, but feeling themselves to be part of a family unit;

- a community made up of married and unmarried people, in established sexual relationships, where the children are nurtured by the community;

- the church family or even...

- members of an organisation or a club, whose feelings for each other are so close that they feel like family.

And there are more. These and other models point to a major shift in society's understanding of modern family life. TV programmes like *Friends* point to this change of emphasis. These days a family isn't simply something that's forced on you by birth, it's also **something you can create** through non-biological relationships.

This is Rob's opinion:

'This sounds awful and very selfish, but I would genuinely prefer to be an orphan! I thought about that a lot as a kid, and still think I would prefer it today. That's mainly because I'm someone that takes responsibility very seriously and I find the family and their problems weigh on me disproportionately to what I get in return from them. In contrast, the Christian family I've become part of has been so much closer and more meaningful in every way than my natural family.'

Most of us have at least two families in our present lives.

'the Christian family... so much closer and more meaningful in every way than my natural family.'

There's our biological inheritance and then there's the family of our choice. Some may have three or more.

This is Karen's experience:

'I think the fact that we live so far from both sets of parents is a hard thing. My parents are two hours away, Tony's almost three. When you want to drop everything and go around for a cup of tea, it's too far. Having said that, the distance can bring advantages too, sometimes (certainly on Tony's side) being close could be really hard. His family have a fabric business that the rest of the family all help in. We are very glad not to be too close to the situation because we could easily be called to take sides or carry the load. The other aspect of our families being far away is that we have developed closer friendships with a few of our congregation who are almost surrogate grandparents. They have given us a nearby shoulder to cry on... volunteer baby-sitting... and lifts to and from meetings when appropriate.'

Karen's story points to three family units:

▪ family of birth

▪ family of marriage

▪ family of profound friendship

For most of us, it's the family of our birth than exerts the most powerful, life-long influences over us. It's the source of

stability

love

mature relationships

practical support

home

It's also the root of:

violence

hatred

insufficiency

instability

emotional coldness

fragmentation

'Digging in the past for me is a bit like overturning stones in the garden.'

Rob's opinion of his biological family and family of choice is clear:

'Personally, I'm untouched by all this interest in family history. Digging in the past for me is a bit like overturning stones in the garden. No treasure — just slugs, woodlice and a smell of decay. The bits I know about by accident are disturbing enough. Lots of adultery. Petty crime. Suicide. Family feuds, bitter, unromantic and senseless. And a worrying amount of mental instability, from obsessive behaviours to hearing voices. Nothing headline-grabbing in itself. But taken as a lump, as a heritage, enough to depress you if you think about it long enough. The best I can claim from the family tree is a sprinkling of eccentrics. There's a definite absence of knights and fair damsels, no wisdom to fall back on, no borrowed fame to claim. No one to be proud of. And no one to lean on, though I've felt the weight of them on me.

'My father was very anti-Christianity and he would storm and rage about me going out to church and sometimes deliberately insist on me doing things for him before I was free to go out on Sundays. We had some huge rows. He told me I was being stupid and grossly deceived as he believed the church was a sort of middle-class club that was really after people's money. He was convinced it was a phase I was going through and told me often that I would grow out of it. If I'd been more mature (I was a very young and naive 18) I suppose I could have coped with this better, but as it was it all just precipitated me moving out of home earlier than I would have done. I invited my parents to my baptism, but they wouldn't come. When I got married there was no question of them contributing in any way. Dad smuggled in bottles of drink (we had the reception in the unlicensed church hall) and spent most of the time skulking outside and smoking.

'For a while there was very little contact with my parents and what there was was very stilted and superficial, otherwise the arguments with dad would erupt again. A year after the wedding we moved even further away from them and the contact was even more fragile. But then when our daughter was born — their first grandchild — we did move back to the same city and mutual attempts were made to resume some kind of relationship. Generally we just avoided talking about Christianity. But it would come up sometimes if he saw things like children's books of Bible stories around. He would accuse us of brainwashing our children. Meanwhile, though I wanted the children to grow up knowing their grandparents, taking them for visits was difficult because of Dad's loud swearing and smoking, and there was never any question of leaving them with them because of our totally opposing values.

'In recent years, when Dad got quite ill, he softened and it was possible to fulfil something of the role of a caring son... but there was always a wariness between us.

'Things have been different with Mum. Over the years when Dad was opposing me she would say nothing. Exactly a year after Dad died things changed quite significantly between us. I had gone with my brother and sisters to mark the anniversary with a family trip to the crematorium and was able to talk quite openly about what death meant to a believer in Christ.

The following day Mum responded positively to going to church with me. She was seventy and I don't think she'd been in a church since she was a small child, apart from weddings and funerals. But from that first Sunday she's hardly missed a week. She is very much part of her local church, is part of the over-60s club and the church coffee morning and has never had so many friends in her life. She still grieves for Dad but she is discovering a whole new way of life. When I go and visit and we go to her church together I have a sense of closeness with her I've never known. She has been able to express her feelings for me — something she had never been able to do before — and although there is still much she doesn't understand about Christianity she is growing in understanding and finds comfort in prayer. This all seems a miracle and in a way some recompense for years of battles with my Dad.

'Struggling with family is one of the reasons that becoming a Christian was such a freeing experience. I don't have to feel shackled to a troupe of apparent no-hopers anymore, even if at times I feel their breath like a chill on my heart. No, I've signed up with the children of God, a family with lots of heroes, sung and unsung, and somehow cleaner credentials.'

God is a family. He is Trinity. Within the unfathomable mystery of oneness, he enjoys the company of a threesome. One undivided substance, three clear relationships. The fifteenth-century Rublev icon from the Eastern Church depicts this astonishing truth, portraying three men eating a meal together. Their body language, posture, position around the table, all indicate that they are intimately joined to each other. It is not just a piece of visual poetry. Alluding to the strange Old Testament story of Abraham and the three visitors, it suggests that God has fellowship within himself and that faith draws us into this unique family of love:

'I've signed up with the children of God, a family with lots of heroes... and somehow cleaner credentials.'

'If anyone loves me, he will obey my teaching. My Father will love him, and we will come to him and make our home with him.' John 14:23

Within the Bible, God reveals himself as having both maternal and paternal instincts:

Can a mother forget the baby at her breast and have no compassion on the child she has borne? Though she may forget, I will not forget you!
Isaiah 49:15

'In that day,' declares the Lord, 'you will call me "my husband"; you will no longer call me "my master".' Hosea 2:16

'O Jerusalem, Jerusalem, you who kill the prophets and stone those sent to you, how often I have longed to gather your children together, as a hen gathers her chicks under her wings, but you were not willing.' Luke 13:34

Jesus didn't come from a privileged background, and neither do many of his followers. Before you can truly appreciate the staggering quantities of faith and filth in Jesus' family tree, one very simple question needs to be asked. Based on the transatlantic success of two television programmes, both involving very different families, ask yourself this question: Does Jesus' family look more like the Simpsons or the Waltons?

Throughout this book you will find two passages repeated in all the various stories. They speak of Jesus' ultimate intentions for his children. Cosmic sentences, encapsulating his infinite love for all his children. Words which identify his desire to take the sting for all the horrors and tragedies of human sin, and rebuild a new community based on forgiveness and purity:

In bringing many sons [and daughters] to glory, it was fitting that God, for whom and through whom everything exists, should make the author of their salvation perfect through suffering. Hebrews 2:10

and

Let us fix our eyes on Jesus, the author and perfecter of our faith, who for the joy set before him endured the cross, scorning its shame, and sat down at the right hand of the throne of God. Hebrews 12:2

He is bringing you to his glory. You were part of the joy that was set before him. During his crucifixion he identified with every person that has ever lived, every sin ever committed. He became that sin, taking the full weight of God's wrath. His own wrath. Too much for us to understand, but what theologian and writer John Stott has termed 'the self substitution of God'. God makes himself responsible for human sin and takes his own punishment. You have been freed at a great price. Priceless freedom. During the sickening crucifixion, mixture of

bones

nails

wire

flesh

nakedness

mockery...

Jesus fixed his eyes on you. He did it all for you. He did it for your family in all its generational vastness.

Chapter 2: dark desires

> ... Judah the father of Perez and Zerah, whose mother was Tamar...

Incest is the complete brutalising of family life. A unit based on mutuality, respect and love is slowly mutilated by **dark secrets**. In order to survive, a family must recognise and celebrate its differences: gender, personality, strengths, weaknesses. Incest breaks every boundary. It invades privacy, manipulates the weak and leaves a trail of generational shame. It is the entry of rape into the home.

Tamar's story is graphic, disturbing and bewildering. Disturbing in that she has intercourse with her father-in-law, conceives and gives birth to twins. Bewildering because she manipulates the intercourse.

Judah, son of Judah, had three sons of his own: Er, Onan and Shelah. Er married Tamar, but their relationship was short-lived. God put him to death, apparently because of his wickedness. Judah then arranged for Onan, his next son, to marry Tamar. According to their culture, it was essential that a married woman conceive and produce children, preferably sons, as soon as possible. It was a sign of divine favour — but it was also an economic necessity; sons would provide for their elderly parents. In Tamar's case, the need for progeny was even more pressing. Widowed at a young age, her childlessness would be construed as a kind of curse, a source of shame. Onan must deliver the goods.

Then Judah said to Onan, 'Lie with your brother's wife and fulfil your duty to her as a brother-in-law to produce offspring for your brother.'

But Onan knew that the offspring would not be his; so whenever he lay with his brother's wife, he spilled his semen on the ground to keep from producing offspring for his brother. What he did was wicked in the Lord's sight; so he put him to death also.
Genesis 38:8-10

He couldn't — or rather he wouldn't. Giving rise to a sin named after him by certain branches of the church, he refused to fully consummate their marriage, withdrawing himself from her vagina before the moment of orgasm. Ejaculating on the floor. Like the hapless Er, Onan too was taken out by God. Judah half considered giving Tamar to Shelah, but Shelah was far too young and their engagement would last a ridiculous length of time.

All this leaves Tamar in limbo land. Unlikely to find a partner beyond her family by marriage, she resorts to **desperate** behaviour. She learns that Judah, her father-in-law, has journeyed to the hill country to visit some relatives and she follows his route. At some point, she realises that Judah uses a certain road regularly. Prostitution. That's what she practices. So immediate and overwhelming is her need for security and a family of her own, she creates a situation in which to have sex with her dead husband's father. Accordingly, she dresses up as a shrine hooker. Local religion was based on numerous 'holy' places, at which priests and prostitutes served. These religions, being highly interactive and participative, encouraged **ritual sex.** Tamar's disguise was therefore not uncommon in that

...she creates a situation in which to have sex with her dead husband's father.

area. Judah turns up, falls for the alluring painted woman and gets her pregnant. He is completely unaware of her true identity. Before they part company, she makes him give her a token, perhaps his belt. Some Bible versions say it is the seal and cord used to sign clay documents. Others talk of a ring. A symbol of his identity, which he gave to her.

Later, back in Judahville, it is brought to his attention that his daughter-in-law is pregnant. Community outrage! And father-in-law's condemnation! Death. Probably by stoning. But before the first rock is skimmed in her direction she produces the belt and its owner realises its import. She lives and gives birth to twins.

This story would be easier if Tamar was a victim and Judah the villain. But they're not. Tamar manipulated sexual intimacy with her father-in-law, who, bereaved and lonely, thought he was having anonymous sex with a foreign prostitute. Who was most guilty? Both were desperate people looking for relief and hope. You could argue that, of the two, she was the most deliberate in her choice and the most aware of the consequences. Unusual. Alarming.

We have no idea how Jesus viewed this skeleton in the cupboard, or any other embarrassment in his family tree. But it's there in black and white. Surprising? Only if you think that the life of Christ was surrounded by perfection, an opinion shared by many people. Jesus was unstained by human failings, therefore his private life was whiter than white. Garbage. From the early years of the Christian faith, his followers had to sort out who he really was. God with clothes on? A perfect spirit who appeared to be human but in reality was God? A group of church leaders, meeting in the city of Chalcedon in 451AD decided to have it out. They concluded that Jesus Christ was possessed of two natures: he was **fully God and fully man**. A little clumsy but expressing a great truth. Many people are brought up to believe that he was more God than man and that his humanity was different to ours. An idea not worth recycling, fit only for the incinerator. In his God-ness he was utterly unlike us but in his humanity he was totally like us. Except he didn't sin. Plenty of opportunities and plenty of choices but he didn't give way. And he had the family from hell.

Meet Caroline. She's a teacher in Ontario, but grew up in England, part of a stable and happy family. Her father kept a café, and business was brisk for six days a week. Except Sundays. On that day, the café was closed and Caroline and her sister went to Sunday School in the morning — and every Sunday afternoon, their cousins would visit them. The eldest cousin was four years older than Caroline. It happened innocently enough, playing a game enjoyed by generations of children: doctors and patients. Simple pleasures betraying pure poison. She the patient, he the doctor. Fondling of the hair, stroking of the belly, brushing of Caroline's secret parts. If there was any innocence, it was short-lived. The cousin's visits, every Sunday, became increasingly abusive. Within a year, Caroline was forced to indulge in fellatio. By the time she was thirteen, her virginity had been crucified. And **all within the family**. And remember this, next door to each monstrous episode, husbands and their wives were playing happy families. They were unaware. They still are.

Somehow, Caroline found faith in Christ. Violated on Sabbath afternoons, but in the morning she attended church. She learned of Jesus, the meek one. Perfect, sinless, sacrificial. His love for her provoked faith and discipleship. But no one told her that he too came from an abusive family, and each Sunday afternoon she endured her own private Calvary.

Later on, after years of suffocating secrecy, she qualified as a teacher, married and moved to Canada. She occasionally flies home for family occasions, where she meets her older cousin.

He too is married and has children. They never speak. He is **terrified of her silence**.

Michael, whose pain was posted on the Internet, has no faith. Caroline's story is grim but she has this in her favour. Within the matrix of her agony, she possesses Christ. Abused by the twisted world of another's mind, she has laid hold of the order that heals. That in Christ all things hold together. Michael has yet to see this:

'Easter is coming up. This year the family will get together at my brother's house. With my problems, I dread the parties. My sisters will be there along with my nieces and great-nieces. Some will be in dresses. I will get sick, mostly from an allergic reaction to something I eat. I tend to think that since this has happened in the past, it will happen again. I will have the symptoms of an allergic reaction without eating the food that I am allergic to. I think of this as accidental conditioning.

'Mothers Day is also coming up. The river was high that day about twenty years ago. The last time I saw my dad he was in the boat bouncing on the water as we sat at the picnic table in our yard. The boat was found the next day upside down about a mile downstream when the river had overflowed its banks. His body was found thirteen days later, after the river had gone down, by some canoeists.

'The way he seemed to be making peace with the family before the trip, among other things, makes me wonder if it might have been suicide.

'Too many triggers for pain. There's a partial memory, apparently of being forced to have oral sex. Even the sight of a man reaching for his zipper in the restroom can trigger my fears. The sight of my own male genitals while urinating has caused me temporary blindness, my sight returning after I zip up. It gets to the point where I just want to take a knife and cut

'I want to take a knife and cut my genitals off.'

my genitals off. More than once a knife I was using has gone flying, to be retrieved after I get things back under control.

'The boy of one of my cousin's may have made things worse for me. He was over visiting one day while I was watching TV. All of a sudden he grabbed at the crotch of my jeans. He then went bragging to his sister that he had touched me. It kind of freaked me out. Visions of me in jail came to my mind, as I thought of the reactions of other adults that might hear him bragging.

'It must have been a couple of years ago that the mechanic at work made a bad comment to me. Just out of the blue he said to me that any of the girls could claim that I raped them after work. Basically, I really freaked. Thoughts of me being locked up as a rapist, unable to defend myself, overcame me. There was one way that I could think of that I could prove I did not or could not rape any girl. I could not rape anyone if I did not have any male genitals. I have thought of dozens of ways to remove the male genitals from my body. I fear that some day I will **lose control.**

'Wearing earrings and nail polish seems to ease things a bit.'

Can anything good come out of abusive relationships? No. Well, that's the normal response, the only one permissible in a sane world. But in the Tamar story, favour came. She produced sons, one of whom was part of the royal line. Thousands of hours later and Jesus comes. This sordid tale is a vital part of the Messiah journey. Jesus would only have been half the man he was without the tale of this desperate young woman and the lonely old man.

So, can anything good come out of abusive relationships?

Good has come to Solomon Kabelu. Solomon's childhood was not happy, due largely to a violent and vindictive father. Each day seemed to bring episodes of beating, punching and verbal abuse. This is how it has affected Solomon:

This sordid tale
is a vital part
of the Messiah
journey.

'When my father left, I was twelve, the eldest child of four. My mother was very upset and struggled to manage, and looking back, I had to be more responsible than most kids of my age and even now I feel I always have to hold everything together and I tend to be over-protective.

'When I became a Christian I was **a b l e   t o   f o r g i v e** my dad for the frequent harsh treatment he had given me. The bitterness I felt from him being away from home for my teenage years went away instantly. I wrote to him and was able to be 'friendly' to him and told him I had become a Christian.

'After being harshly treated in my childhood by my father, it has made me very careful not to use violence towards my children or wife. Because I was treated badly, I think that working as a children's pastor for some years has been an expression of wanting to care for and show God's love and protection for children.'

Another story of abuse. A pastor serves faithfully, loyally and well. Visionary, an able preacher, many come to faith through him. Trusted confidant, sought-after counsellor. At the same time he's having an affair with a woman in his own church, conducting secret liaisons in various hotels on ministry trips. On one such trip, in Scotland, they book into a hotel, enjoying the days together, while he holds revival meetings in a nearby church. One evening, a young man attends the nightly meeting, curious, thirsty to know more of God, tired with the compromise in his own life. As the evening progresses he feels greatly disturbed with the man in the expensive suit and flash tie. Clearly, almost audibly, with the clarity of a WAP phone, he hears this from God: 'He is having an affair and is staying in a hotel with a woman who is not his wife.' He even hears the name of the hotel and the room number. The following day, after a restless night, he summons his courage and goes to the hotel, climbs the stairs and knocks on the door. The minister appears, casually dressed, mildly surprised. Young man doesn't know how to start the conversation, almost drowns in whirlpool stammerings. But he believes the voice more than the man whom he now faces. 'I, I, hope you don't mind, but, I, think God has given me a message, kind of thing for you.' Then he said it: 'You are having an affair and the woman who is with you now is not your wife.' Silence. The minister slams the door in his face. A sordid business. Yet one in which God shows his power, speaks through one of his children.

So many abuses of power within intimate relationships. Manipulation, domination and control combine to make a poisonous trinity, symbiotic companions who poison relationships. Like

- the social worker who abused children in his care for a period of twenty years;

- the doctor who murdered over a hundred patients, persuading many of them, before their death, to change their wills in his favour;

- the sister who persuaded her elderly father to leave the family home to her, instead of her older sister. She has systematically seen to it that her sister and family have been deprived of any possible inherited material gain.

Abuse, and lots of it.

Tamar's story with all its bewildering contemporaneity, reminds us that women and children are often the most vulnerably-placed in family life.

Enshrined in diverse cultures are customs which enslave and degrade. Just two examples:

■ Until the early years of the twentieth century, UK children were expected to work long hours in hard manual labour.

■ Until a hundred years ago, women in China had their feet bound, forced to wear excruciatingly uncomfortable shoes in order to achieve a certain posture and deportment.

In contrast, sometimes it is mothers who speak out against institutional and therefore unnoticed abuse. The USA's gun laws allow for the widespread ownership and sale of firearms. After a spate of violent gun deaths against children, a massive march of mothers representing dozens of different religious groups descended on Washington DC, protesting against such laws, voicing their fears for their own children. Here's one news report:

More than 50 faith groups participated in the Million Mom March, an event which attracted 500,000 people to the US capital on 14 May, Mothers Day, to demand tougher laws on the ownership and use of guns.

In addition, smaller marches took place in more than 65 cities across the US.

Across the sea of marchers — mostly women — were many banners and posters identifying individual congregations and denominational groups.

Many mass killings, including some at schools, have made gun ownership one of the most controversial issues in the US. While gun owners and manufacturers insist that every citizen has a right to self-defence, and thus to have access to firearms, opponents point to statistics showing huge numbers of deaths brought about by a proliferation of gun ownership. According to statistics released at the march, in 1997 a total of 32,436 people in the US were killed by guns:

- 17,566 were suicides

- 13,522 were homicides

- 981 were accidental shootings

- 367 were shooting deaths of undetermined intent

Nelda Gray, a member of Kirkwood United Methodist Church in Kirkwood, Missouri, said she attended the march because she wanted to be part of important social change. 'The most remarkable part was hearing the mothers of young murder victims talk about their losses,' she said. 'In America, it seems gun rights are taken more seriously than people's rights.'

A retired professional counsellor, Gray, said she knew first-hand the dangers of guns in the lives of the mentally ill and mentally disabled. 'I'm very aware of what happens when guns get in the hands of people who are off their medication or those under the influence of alcohol and drugs,' she said. 'Conflict resolution isn't going to happen when there's a gun present.'

Debi Holon, a mother of three teenagers and a member of the United Methodist Church in Sayreville, New Jersey, said she attended the march because it finally seemed like a chance to be heard on something that's been bothering her for years. 'As one speaker said, "You just get tired of yelling at the TV".' she said, referring to violence on television.

'I hope this is a kick-off for greater action to come,' she said. 'As soon as I get a chance, I'm going to find a local group wanting to continue this. And I'm going to vote for the people who support gun control.'

Chapter 3: savage genes

For every abusive act there's a corresponding secret. Judah kept quiet about his assignation with a foreign prostitute, pleased that no one had noticed. Confronted by Tamar's sexual compromise, his attitude couldn't be more unsympathetic. Death by stoning, that's what she deserved. Religious killing. Hypocrisy, injustice, that's the cry of the unjust. Whether it's Victorian gentlemen pontificating on Sunday and fornicating on Monday, or religious children's homes papering over generations of paedophilia with ritual prayer. The result is the same. Veils, cloaks, hoods, blinds and masks keep the balance, sometimes for good. Many a vile secret has crowed in the midnight hour only to die in hideous anonymity. Too many Judahs have escaped judgement.

But this Judah was strangled by his own belt. Or unmasked by his signet ring. His gift token became the means of his disclosure. Tamar's shrewdness exposed Judah's sin, causing him to **fall from the moral high ground** into the slum of public dishonesty. Again the text doesn't explore the process leading up to this exposure. The story, as written, explains the events in a factual and dispassionate way. Tamar dresses up as a foreign prostitute and has sexual relations with her father-in-law. So what? The passage however leads us to draw at least two conclusions.

- She knew what she was doing — intending to conceive and force Judah to acknowledge her as his wife.

■ He wanted to escape the consequences of his lapse.

But we know nothing of the emotional process. Before the final twist, Tamar was as good as dead. Her timing was immaculate. How did she feel about naming and shaming her father-in-law? Speaking of Judah, how did he react when his cloak of respectability was torn away by Tamar's accusations? Silence. As with many other Old Testament passages describing moral failure, the narrative is curiously stark.

■ **Abraham**, on several occasions, lies about the nature of his relationship with Sara, his wife. No reprimand follows.

■ **Jacob** lies to virtually everyone in his family and receives no rebuke from on high.

■ Prime Minister **Joseph** manipulates his brothers and father before finally disclosing his identity to them all.

There are, of course, many other stories where God's displeasure is kindled by moral lapses. But it's as though the Bible is saying **that human collapse is normal.** Regrettable, consequential, spiritually divisive, socially fragmenting, but normal. Worse, several Bible characters pass on their flaws to succeeding generations, often in a more concentrated form:

■ Rebellion by **Adam** finds violent expression in Cain.

■ **David**, after his adulterous relationship, produces sons who create civil war.

■ **Jacob**, the liar, has six sons who lied about attempted fratricide and one who is unbearably vain.

The Old Testament's view of family weakness is that it reproduces itself in the lives of limited generations, although **God's blessing has infinite repercussions for good.**

> ...I the Lord your God, am a jealous God, punishing the children for the sin of the fathers to the third and fourth generation of those who hate me, but showing love to a thousand generations of those who love me and keep my commandments. <u>Exodus 20: 5,6</u>

Unfashionable, incomprehensible, uncomfortable. Our age doesn't understand generational sin, but it does pride itself on its knowledge of genes. The human genome project has been mapped at the dawn of the new millennium and greeted by huge international acclaim. Likening it to 'the book of life', and 'the Bible', scientists in Britain, Europe and the US have deciphered the three-billion-letter DNA alphabet that shapes and limits human existence. Were it typed, single-spaced, on A4 paper, the blueprint for a single human would fill 750,000 pages. It is hoped that this chromosome code will help eliminate inherited diseases that have scarred generations of families:

- muscular dystrophy
- Huntingdon's chorea
- cystic fibrosis
- porphyria
- haemophilia
- diabetes
- and hundreds of others.

This majestic project offers wonderful hope to those trapped in inherited disease. It also predicts a more

disturbing future. Princeton biologist, Lee Silver, foresees a world 350 years from now, where pressure from affluent parents will have influenced gene and cloning technology to alarming extremes. Society will be divided into two classes: 90% 'naturals' and 10% 'gene enriched', the latter forming a modern-day hereditary class of **genetic aristocrats**. This latter group is so different to the former that they are effectively another species.

Interestingly, some philosophers and theologians have begun to apply human genome logic to other human realities, apart from disease. Some have posited an inherited basis for:

> sexual promiscuity
> love
> religion
> crime

Not a matter of moral judgement but of biological inevitability.

I know someone with an interesting story. Brought up in a non-church-going family, Alison knew little of God and virtually nothing about Jesus. Leaving home to pursue nurse training, she met a number of Christians whose way of life appealed to her. She reasoned that if these followers of Jesus were such agreeable people, then their master must be even more inspiring. She researched his life, asked questions, realised that he'd died for her and that he was presently alive. She received him into her life.

A few years later and monstrous calamity struck her family. Alison's mother died of breast cancer, as did her twin sister. During her sister's final days, Alison would often accompany the specialist palliative care nurse in visiting her.

These two nurses got to know each other very well. This is a snippet of one of their conversations:

'This is very hard for me to say, and you probably know it already, but it's likely that you'll get breast cancer. You should get yourself screened as soon as possible.'

Alison hesitates. How to reply? In a faltering voice:

'I became a Christian a few years ago and I've come to realise something. There have been times when I've been terrified of getting cancer, but know now that I don't have to live in the fear of it. I believe that in asking Jesus into my life, I've entered a new family. God is my father and he's forgiven my past sins and **I don't have to be ruled by my family's genes.**'

Whacky? Crazy? Spiritually unhinged? She's still alive and she still hasn't had cancer.

Jesus' genes were contaminated — you might say, science aside — by the nasty detritus of incest. His chromosomes bore the echo of a twisted one-night stand. You could say, bravely, that his genes weren't perfect.

In the empty cross and abandoned tomb there's mercy for every Judah and every Tamar. Present in Jesus there's

> **judgement** on vicious sexual acts
> **deep forgiveness** for those who'll
> take it and
> **power** to move on

Jesus wasn't defined by his darkest gene pool. For him, life was flooded by a vision of his Father's glory. All stare but no glare. Strangely, he embraced

> the lethal injection
>
> electric chair
>
> guillotine

Jesus wasn't defined by his darkest gene pool.

axe

hangman's noose

gas chamber

death camp...

...namely death by crucifixion. This God-man who fled away from abusive relationships and encouraged his followers to do the same, died a victim of abuse. Except that the Bible doesn't portray it that way. Jesus' death was a deliberate act on his part. Calculated, planned, foreseen, **chosen**. In the bizarre folly of his slaughter, Jesus believed that he was setting the abusers and their victims free. Unbelievable horror that a young innocent, virgin should make himself responsible, before God and his heaven, for every monstrous abusive deed. I believe that in the savage garden of Gethsemane and the piercing migraine of Skull Hill, this passionate Messiah

wept in the Bosnian death camps

sucked for air in the chambers of Auchwitz

suffered rape at the hands of a kindly uncle

howled with fear into the midnight sky

entered Tamar's strange world

made Judah's cloak his own

See, my servant will act wisely;
       he will be raised and lifted up and highly exalted.
Just as there were many who were appalled at him —
his appearance was so disfigured beyond that of any man
       and his form marred beyond human likeness —

so he will sprinkle many nations,
    and kings will shut their mouths because of
him.
For what they were not told, they will see,
    and what they have not heard, they will
understand.'
Isaiah 52:13-15

And read this again:

In bringing many sons [and daughters] to
glory, it was fitting that God, for whom and
through whom everything exists, should make
the author of their salvation perfect through
suffering. Hebrews 2:10

And marvel at this:

...who for the joy set before him, endured the
cross, scorning its shame, and sat down at the
right hand of the throne of God.' Hebrews
12:2

Jesus wants to bring all the Tamars and all the Judahs into
glory with him.

Chapter 4:a true pro

We're returning to the opening of Matthew's Gospel to pick up again on that family tree of Jesus:

Ram the father of Amminadab, Amminadab the father of Nashon, Nashon the father of Salmon, Salmon the father of Boaz, whose mother was Rahab... Matthew 1:4,5

Rahab was a Canaanite hooker. She lived in the fortified city of Jericho and, presumably, was good at her job. Jericho was an established and prosperous community, almost as ancient as the world's oldest profession. Part of a powerful country, it had enjoyed centuries of affluence and national strength. It was a good place to live. If you were a prostitute it meant a steady stream of merchants, pilgrims and travellers. **Easy living for good time girls.**

But God had a disturbing plan. Annihilation. Out in the desert beyond the river that marked Canaan's border, God's people had roamed aimlessly for forty years. Two leaders later, the longest detour in history and their sandy trek was about to end. Moses, the Israelites' first leader, had promised a land flowing with milk and honey, but he himself never saw it. A fit of petulance disqualified him before God. The second leader, Joshua, was equally visionary. He could see beyond the river. He saw the land and the city. Jericho was a tumbling certainty. Taking an epic number of people through a torrid river was no easy task, especially as it involved transporting a holy box. But they did it, thanks to a miracle. The waves rolled back like prayer mats and the men, women, children, animals, priests and their holy box, walked through.

They camped for a few nights on the Canaanite side. Joshua sent a couple of spies to eye the exotic Jericho. The two men entered the city but feared for their lives, terrified that they might be recognised and killed. They looked different, maybe with darker skin or certain distinguishing facial features.

Looking for accommodation, they somehow arrived at a brothel. This was Rahab's house. Of all the buildings in this substantial city, they chose this one. Maybe it was an accident, but maybe not. Away from the constraints of family, far from Joshua and the holy box, perhaps they wanted to indulge in a little sin. Most men, when staying at a bordello, are not heard to remark on the quality of the decor or the elegant cuisine. Of course, they may have been weary travellers who took no notice of their whereabouts, desperate for a good night's sleep.

Excuse me?

In the morning, came the verbal bombshell. Jericho, the men announced, was soon to be razed to the ground by a tribe of displaced refugees. Rahab struck a bargain: I've put you up for the night, the least you can do is save me and my household. They agreed to protect her, providing she did one thing and fix **a red scarf** to her window ledge. This she did and survived the destruction.

Strange story.

Some women

    don't like being mothers

      enjoy having many lovers

Some people have mixed feelings about their own mothers.

I know a mother who met her son last year. Sylvia grew up in one of Amsterdam's less affluent neighbourhoods. Ordinary childhood, moderately gifted, she eventually trained as a nurse in one of the city's teaching hospitals. Raised in a religious household, she wasn't especially spiritual, although she dutifully attended a small exclusive sect each Sunday. Eventually she left Amsterdam, gaining her first post in a hospital in Utrecht. Lodging in the home of a local pastor, she got on with a new life in a new city. In the midst of it all, she met a young policeman at a staff dance and this sexually innocent young woman fell for the man in a uniform. Clumsy kisses on the dance floor led to furtive fumblings in the car park and finally to consummation in the car. They **never met again.** Except this. Within a few weeks she realised that she was pregnant. And when you need one, there isn't a policeman to be found.

Amazingly, Sylvia didn't tell her parents. And the pastor, although supportive, exuded judgement. There could only be one conclusion and it bore no relation to Sylvia's own feelings. Adoption. No sooner had the baby boy's umbilicus been **severed** than she was wrenched away from her new creation, leaving her to the rest of her life.

Eric travelled. Before the age of two years he'd already had three homes; two in the Netherlands before finally being adopted by a family in London. Bright, musical, gifted, creative, Eric enjoyed a rich and prosperous home life as he grew. Except this. He felt as though he carried **a black hole within him** all the time. Unusually sensitive, frequently prone to minor illness, Eric spent much of his adolescence in academic achievement and inward brooding. By age 21 Eric had trained as a professional musician, earning his living through private tuition and public performance. A few years later and he married, children arriving within a short time.

Becoming a father triggered **the emotional subsidence** he had long feared. Assured of his own offspring's history, he now dreaded his own. He wanted roots, **a home for his genes**, but all he had was a vague Dutch connection. After a series of strange depressive illnesses, his adopted father sensed Eric's true agony and began some furtive detective work. All he knew was Eric's mother's maiden name and, of course, he had the birth certificate.

Correspondence, phone calls, web surfing yielded nothing. Amsterdam is a large and mobile city. By chance he learned of an agency which helps adopted children find their birth parents. Further research resulted in dozens of leads, each one a cul-de-sac. Nothing. Finally, one wet, grey, autumn Saturday afternoon, Eric's dad received a phone call. 'I've found her. She lives in Antwerp and her married name is de Hoogh. Sylvia de Hoogh.' End of information. Uncertain of his next move, he decided not to tell Eric. It could mean yet more disappointment. Tentatively, he held the telephone receiver and rang the Belgian number. Answered by a man. Awkward. Eric's English disturbed the Belgian familiarity, introducing a strange note.

'Yes, Mrs de Hoogh does live here.'

'May I speak to her.'

'Of course, I'll bring her to the phone.'

Silence.

'It's about my son, isn't it.'

Silence.

'Yes... umm... how did you know?'

'I've been waiting for this phone call for the past 34 years.'

He wanted roots,
a home for
his genes.

Eric and Sylvia met last year. For the first time since his birth. Eric has been introduced to his mother and two sisters. And his twin brother. Both brothers are professional musicians and both suffer the same medical disorders.

Every day since his birth, Sylvia has wept for her abandoned son. Permitted by the legal authorities to keep one of the twins, she arbitrarily chose Johann. Shortly after this trauma, she jettisoned the pinched and mean religion of her childhood, maintaining a private faith. Eventually she married an architect, who was a devout Catholic. Every day she visited her parish church, lit a candle and prayed for Eric, the name she'd given him at his birth.

After Rahab's miraculous deliverance, her reputation must have been legendary. But this is the question. Was she known as a woman of great faith? Or a lucky prostitute? Yes, she would have acquired a reputation. Been given names.

Reputation. What they, the family, say about us. The names given to us are **very powerful**, shaping our thought and life patterns. This is Monica's story:

'From when I was little my dad always called me Lady Muck. By that he meant I never thought my family was good enough for me, that I was always trying to get 'above myself'. I don't know where I got ideas of self-improvement from, but it's true, I was always trying to make life better. The house was always dirty and even as a young kid I would try to clean it up — and then dad would call me Lady Muck. I was always reporting facts and bits of good advice that my teacher told me — and then dad would call me Lady Muck. I worked hard at school and with my teacher's encouragement I passed the entrance exam to a girls' grammar school that only took the top two per cent of girls in the city. And Dad called me Lady Muck. That name-calling hammered a wedge between me and my family. I always felt different, as if I didn't belong.

'But the name he called my youngest sister was worse. He called her 'The Queer One'. By this he meant she was strange, not quite right in the head. The truth was she was a shy, timid child, prone to dreaminess and quietness. She would hide behind my mum, terrified of him and his loud ways. His clumsy teasing banter — which produced defiance in me and laughter in my next sister — always reduced her to tears, which he took as a sign of weakness, where it was really sensitivity. His name calling of her and his treatment of her paralysed her. She grew up totally lacking in self-confidence. Not a shred of self-esteem. She married very young, to a version of my dad, someone loud and opinionated and domineering. And of course the marriage didn't last.

'And when I look at her I see the anxieties of a hard life etched on her face, and I feel Dad was much to blame.

'I've tried never to label my own kids, even with nick-names. I know they're powerful things.'

Powerful things. So powerful that God has a habit of re-naming his children:

In the place where it was said to them, 'You are not my people', they will be called 'sons of the Living God'. Hosea 1:10

I know someone who was told by his dad that he'd never be any good at mathematics. His siblings had been useless at it, so he said, as had his mum and dad. Strangely, when this man had his own children, he refused to pass on this self-destructing prophecy and his own children have dazzled in the subject.

I know someone else whose childhood was punctuated by outbreaks of family mayhem. But it was also marked by frequent vocal reminders that she was loved, valued, cherished. Today, she is characterised by a spirit of security and peace, even though her life has not been an easy one.

I will say to those called 'Not my people', 'You are my people'; and they will say, 'You are my God.' **Hosea 2:23**

To him who overcomes, I will give some of the hidden manna. I will also give him a white stone with a new name written on it, known only to him who receives it. **Revelation 2:17**

Naming is as old as the human family. Adam was entrusted by God to order his world through language. It's an ancient ceremony. Most churches have special acts of worship associated with new-born babies. These differ in theological significance, but each involves thanksgiving to God for new life and the bestowing of a name. This is taken from the Church of England's *Book of Common Prayer*:

> *Then the Priest shall take the child into his hands, and shall say to the Godfathers and Godmothers, Name this child. And then naming it after them (if they shall certify him that this child may well endure it), he shall dip it in the water discreetly and warily, saying,*

> *'N, I baptise thee in the Name of the Father, and of the Son, and of the Holy Spirit. Amen'*

Most of the time, debates about baptism rage around the issues of practice and custom. Sad, since this quaint injunction makes a profound connection: baptism is the sinking of my name into the Unnamed Name. God's name and reputation originates within himself. His name gives meaning to ours. **Our true identity** as individuals and families can only be fully known in so far as we recognise God's loving authority in our lives:

For this reason I kneel before the Father, from whom his whole family in heaven and on earth derives its name. **Ephesians 3:14,15**

We have a terrifying power to mould our world according to our image. How will we map this world unless we have seen a purer vision?

Two interesting stories.

At the end of the nineteenth century, maps of the world were coloured according to colonial interests. Pink was the hue to be seen in. This designated the British Empire. At some point, it was decided to complete a map of Ireland, then under UK sovereignty. Government officials toured the country, renaming the entire topography. Dissent was crushed on the basis that English was the language of power and superiority.

My grandfather grew up in West Wales at the end of nineteenth century. Welsh was the language of home and chapel, and it was only natural that it should also be the language of the school playground. Many Welsh people couldn't speak English and had no need to. But teachers who shared the same language and lived in the same streets were required, by law, to stamp out the use of Welsh in state schools. Those caught speaking in the Celtic tongue were humiliated by the wearing of the 'Welsh Not'. This cumbersome pendant hung around the wearer's neck, proclaiming to all that he had been guilty of breaking the law in speaking a forbidden language. Named both as a law breaker and language terrorist.

God has an agenda for the badly named. It's called **exaltation.** Giving the poor, wretched and bullied a reputation that's been denied them. More. He's also decreed that those whose good name rests on wealth, power, influence, will, one day, be forgotten. Mary, the mother of Jesus was moved to sing a magnificent song when she realised that God was on her side:

> My soul glorifies the Lord and my spirit rejoices in God my Saviour, for he has been mindful of the humble state of his servant. From now on all generations will call me blessed, for the Mighty One has done great things for me - holy is his name.
> Luke 1:46-49

She's rejoicing in her **new name** on the basis that she has realised the wonderful greatness of his. But there's more...

> ...he has scattered those who are proud in their inmost thoughts. He has brought down rulers from their thrones but has lifted up the humble. Luke 1:51,52

Come the second coming revolution, it would be wise to have heeded James's sharp words:

> Now listen, you rich people, weep and wail because of the misery that is coming upon you. Your wealth has rotted, and moths have eaten your clothes. Your gold and silver are corroded. Their corrosion will testify against you and eat your flesh like fire. You have hoarded wealth in the last days. Look! The wages you failed to pay the workmen who mowed your fields are crying out against you. The cries of the harvesters have reached the ears of the Lord Almighty. You have lived on earth in luxury and self-indulgence. You have fattened yourselves in the day of slaughter. You have condemned and murdered innocent men, who were not opposing you. James 5:1-6

Traditional Indian society is extremely hierarchical. Based on the Hindu idea of reincarnation, people's advance through the hierarchy depends on the level of moral goodness achieved in past lives. At the top of the caste pile sit the Brahmin, and the Dalits sit at the bottom. The latter are known as 'the untouchables', whose presence is so unclean that their company is shunned. They are outcasts, frequently suffer poverty and ill health, denied access to education. But a powerful and radical appointment has been made, **challenging the fatalism of bad names**. Read the report:

Marampudi Joji made history on 30 April when he became the first Dalit archbishop in the Roman Catholic Church in India.

Joji was installed as Archbishop of Hyderabad, capital of the state of Andhra Pradesh in southern India, where he is now the leader of 90,000 Catholics. Ironically, however, the installation of Archbishop Joji was conducted by his predecessor, Archbishop Samineni Arulappa, who only weeks before caused much controversy by criticising Joji's appointment in what some have seen as veiled prejudice against Dalits. Despite this, the installation went smoothly, and Archbishop Arulappa urged all present to co-operate fully with the new archbishop. The elevation of the 57-year-old Dalit bishop — one of three Dalits in the 180-strong Catholic Bishops' Conference of India (CBCI) — to the rank of archbishop is an important event for his church and for the entire Christian community of India. More than 60 per cent of the nation's 16 million Catholics are Dalits; in Andhra Pradesh state more than 80 per cent of Christians are Dalits.

Once treated as "untouchables" in the India's caste-dominated society, Dalits (meaning "trampled upon" in Sanskrit) are even today often treated as "social outcasts" forced to live outside the rigid four-tier hierarchy of castes which Hindus believe has divine approval.

Recent tragic events in Britain have indicated an equally destructive form of bad naming. **Racism**. The Stephen Lawrence Inquiry centred on a brutal murder in South London in the late 1990s. Stephen Lawrence, a black youth, was attacked and killed by a gang of white men in the street. No arrests followed and therefore no prosecution. Stephen's parents campaigned tirelessly for years to secure justice for their son's murder, eventually gaining an admission from the Metropolitan Police that it had been guilty of 'institutional racism.'

Many social commentators fear that the UK and other western countries are witnessing an resurgence of racism. Surprising, therefore, that the appointment of the new President of the UK Methodist conference in 2000 refreshingly bucks this depressing trend. The Rev Inderjit Bhogal comes from an immigrant Sikh family, but discovered faith in Christ as a young man. After his induction to his new position, he spoke about the compelling nature of Jesus Christ, saying 'the genius of Jesus was to put food, a meal, at the centre of his community.' He went on to add that the nation and the church can be judged by how we treat the elderly, children and strangers. 'What for example, is our nation's treatment of those who seek refuge and asylum here — today's strangers?' Mr Bhogal went on: 'The situation is now scandalous...The abusive ways in which asylum seekers are treated mocks the image of God in their human being...Theology begins where we ask, Why is it like this? Spirituality begins with an honesty about reality.'

Rahab may have attracted some name calling, may have had a bad reputation, but, strangely, she may have been a woman of faith. Celebrated in Jesus' odd family tree, she reminds us that the family of faith is as bizarre as every other. Except that God invites the broken, wounded, screwed up and

> 'Spirituality begins with an honesty about reality.'
> – Inderjit Bhogal

compromised to taste his forgiveness, on one condition. That they will abandon the toxins they have enjoyed and accept a new power **and a new name.** All change.

Hear it again:

Let us fix our eyes on Jesus, the author and perfecter of our faith, who for the joy set before him endured the cross, scorning its shame, and sat down at the right hand of the throne of God. **Hebrews 12:2**

Within the torment of his final death rattle, Jesus set his eye on Rahab and loved her. His blood and water are thicker than anyone else's and he covered her with his poured-out life. In his death you, too, can close down **poisonous patterns,** the influence of names and reputations. And in his resurrection you too can feel the stirrings of his new life, living through you.

I once met someone who used to be a call girl. Working in Central London, she had numerous male clients and generated enough income to buy a flat overlooking the capital's Regents Park. Her schedule was demanding, for most days she engaged in intercourse on the hour, every hour. She prided herself on having purchased an expensive way of life: 'I only wear Rolex and Versace, dear,' she once said to me.

Until she fell in love. Not with one of her clients, but, ironically, with a man she met in her local Coin-Op Launderette. Not exactly love at first wash, but almost. Conversation, meal in a wine bar, clubbing. But no sex. He didn't push it and neither did she. She loved his company, surprised to find out that he was a Christian. Described how he had come to trust in Jesus and how he had been 'baptised in the Spirit', as he put it. Invited her to his church, in one of London's outer suburbs, where a visiting American preacher was ministering each night. She went. Took time off. Apprehensive, she didn't like the sound of 'visiting American preacher', but she really liked her new friend. Fearful, very fearful, of what might God do to her. **Her, of all people.**

Prostitutes and pulpits don't normally share the same room. He spoke, and his manner was mild, understated, generous. She liked him. At the end of his talk, he invited everyone to stand and simply said: '**Come, Holy Spirit.**' Silence. More silence, but he didn't seem bothered. Then someone fell, another cried, a few laughed, more weeping. He began to speak, describing people's lives as though he knew them. People came forward for prayer. She left — bewildered, excited, overwhelmed. Arriving back at her flat, she collapsed onto her bed and lay silently. Knowing nothing about God or the church, she repeated the words she'd heard earlier: '**Come, Holy Spirit.**' This is how she described the experience:

'Almost immediately, I felt something like an electric shock pass through me and it seemed to go on for ages. What was really strange was that this electricity seemed to focus on my private parts. As though my body was being cleansed. I then started crying, feeling that I was **living a cheap and dirty life**. I didn't know Jesus then, but I knew that this was God **and he wanted to forgive me**. I started talking to him. It went on for ages.'

The following day she visited her new friend, who explained Jesus to her, and her need to confess her sin, repent, and receive his forgiveness. The Holy Spirit would then come and live inside her. She did. And he does.

'I felt something like an electric shock pass through me... As though my body was being cleansed.'

Chapter 5: mixed-up marriages

...Boaz the father of Obed, whose mother was
Ruth... <u>Matthew Chapter 1:5</u>

'I'm a wealthy man. But until a few years back I was lonely and loaded. Life had been good to me, favoured me with property, servants, prosperity. But no one to share it all with.

'Family, for me, is very important. For my nation **it's the foundation of everything.** My people regard the family unit as God's primary way of ordering society. Surrounded by people, relatives, friends, but I had no soulmate.

'There was my mother, of course. She kept tabs on me constantly, preying into my thoughts, friendships, business affairs. 'It's only because I love you, darling', was her mantra, but it really annoyed me. I was 35, for goodness sake!

'Exotic, that's what you'd probably call her. You can tell from the colour of her skin that she's not part of the ancient tribes. Slightly darker, taller, lighter hair. She can talk the hind legs off a he-goat but there's one sure way of quietening her. Talk about her past. She won't, or not very often. And only then to close friends or family.

'It's an amazing story. As far as I can make out she spent most of her earlier life in Jericho city, just east of the Jordan. In those days, the Canaanites ran everything. It was their land, and I always imagine she worked for the religion service. A kind of priestess, although her daily rituals would be frowned upon these days. As well as leading worship to various gods, she had to offer her body to male worshippers. This is how it worked. They'd come to the main shrines in Jericho, at different times in the year, in order to worship Baal, and others. Mostly, Baal, he was the chief god. They believed that their gods could help them get good harvests, especially if they had sex with women of proven fertility. Basically, if you screwed a priestess, the gods would mate with each other (don't ask me how!) and the whole world would be fertile. So, yes, my mother was a prostitute...

'One night she was visited by a couple of strangers, spies sent out by the leader of the time, Joshua. She says it was one of them who became my father, and that women know these things... well, it would be hard to prove. Few days later every building collapsed, and virtually everyone in Jericho was killed. Felt like an earthquake, that's what my mother said. Must have been ghastly. Except it wasn't really an earthquake but an invasion... but there was no real army, according to my mother. Because after the dust had settled, all that could be seen were a group of people holding drums, tambourines, lyres and the terrifying box we call the Ark of the Covenant. People said they simply sang the place down, singing the songs of Yahweh!

'We survived. No one else did. Every street was destroyed, and the people killed. Nothing about my family history survived that holocaust... except for this one thing. In my parents' bedroom there's a small bronze box, which my mother keeps locked for most of the year. It's only opened when we celebrate the Passover and then she wears her greatest treasure. **A red scarf**. Fading with the passage of time, and stained with the tears of many years, mother gets it out and fingers and strokes it, sort of tenderly.

'Where was I? Yes, as I said, I was lonely. Jewish girls are OK, but I hadn't found one I really liked. You know... the chemistry

'...yes, my mother was a prostitute...'

thing. My religion doesn't really allow me to marry from other races. Believe me, that's hard when you're around different people all the time. I'd pretty much given up on ever getting married and having children, thought I'd work at building up my business. And that's what I did.

'Until I met her. Ruth. What you might call love in a blur! My long distance isn't brilliant, but I noticed a different shape, garment colour, working in one of my fields. It was harvest time. After one of the early shifts, I overheard the women gossiping about a couple of beggars, one of whom was a young gentile woman. I guessed it was her and instructed my workers not to be too precise in their harvesting. "Leave some leftovers for the strangers," I said to them. Knowing that I'm quite religious, they didn't quibble. At least not to my face. Our law commands us to pay special regard to any strangers in our midst, even if they are foreigners.

'I was so curious to meet her that I tracked her down one morning in the fields and gave her permission to take all the corn she wanted, enough for herself and her mother-in-law.

'She's beautiful! Moabites are our sworn enemies but I thought she was irresistible!

'Nothing happened for a few weeks, but then everything changed one night. Party time, and one of those long summer evenings when the food is excellent and the wine even better. I admit I'd drunk too much and fell into bed in the early hours, very mellow.

'Then at one point in the night, I woke — and found Ruth with me, lying at my feet. She seemed a bit afraid, but I asked her to stay, on condition that she left early in the morning. I didn't want my men gossiping that I'd spent the night with a foreign whore.

'What was she doing there? Good question, especially if you're not from around here. Let me explain. We've got a custom that allows us to buy the property of dead relatives. It's a total liability, actually, inasmuch that if you buy the land you become responsible for any slaves, servants, animals etc. And wives. You become what's called **a kinsman redeemer**, giving financial security and freedom to your family. In coming to my bed, Ruth wasn't making some kind of cheap pass at me, she was asserting her legal right to my protection. Believe me, nothing happened that shouldn't have!

'Now, I'm not directly related to Ruth, but I am from the same family as her mother-in-law, Naomi. After she'd been widowed, Naomi came back looking for a member of her family, hoping to find someone who'd care for her. Ruth joined her, preferring her potential new family and their God above her own.

'The day after Ruth slept at my feet, I approached the one man I knew who had stronger family links with Naomi. I explained her position. Widow, owned land in the vicinity, would he like to buy the land as her kinsman redeemer? At first, he agreed. But as soon as I laid out the terms of the deal he retracted. The land was attractive — but he didn't want a dead man's wife and her foreign girl eating into his pay roll. "You redeem her", were his words to me. I did and asked Ruth to marry me. You cannot believe how happy I was when she agreed!

'A Jew and a Moabitess! Sure, it's a mixed marriage, and some don't approve. But Ruth is an exceptional, courageous woman. Her history is not mine and her nation is despised by most of the people I know — but I don't care, she has given me so much joy! She's also given me children. Just as was prophesied. Before we got married, the old men of the village said these words:

May the Lord make the woman who is coming into your home like Rachel and Leah, who together built up the house of Israel. May you have standing in Ephrathah and be famous in Bethlehem. Through the offspring the Lord gives you by this young woman, may your family be like that of Perez, whom Tamar bore to Judah. Ruth 4:11,12

Mixed marriages: Ruth and Boaz; Tom and Jane; Paolo and Beth.

'I've looked into all this and discovered that Leah and Rachel were both wives of Jacob, one of my ancestors. Not a great man, by all accounts. But Leah and Rachel gave Jacob twelve sons, including Judah, who I think was my great-great-great-great-great grandfather. It was Rachel who gave him Joseph. Now, he really was a great man. His brothers sold him to some Egyptian travellers and thought they'd got rid of him. That one event was a dramatic turning point in the history of my people. Eventually, they all landed up in Egypt and stayed there for about 400 years.

'Let them say what they like about Ruth and me. My family isn't up to much, anyway. My mother was a prostitute, Jacob was a small-time crook and cheat. And then there's Judah! Enough said. No one ever mentions him, probably because he slept with his own daughter-in-law. I'm happy I've got Ruth — but, believe me, nothing good will ever come out of this family.'

Ruth and Boaz had a mixed marriage. Such partnerships are not easy. The fusion of different cultures, colours and sometimes religions can create **conflict and estrangement** from other family members. Like Jane and Tom.

Jane is white and grew up in the south east of England. Tom is black and Jamaican. They met during one of Jane's holidays in the West Indies. It was a Sunday and she was visiting one of the island's many churches They met during the church lunch, to which all visitors had been invited. Both were immediately attracted to each other. Drawn together by strong chemistry and shared Christian faith, they were inseparable for the rest of Jane's holiday.

Tom proposed marriage to Jane on her final day and she accepted. She returned home an engaged woman, much to the tepid dismay of her family. Six months later they were married in the Caribbean and they made their first home in Kent. Almost immediately there were problems. Jane's family had become increasingly uneasy at her marrying a black man, and Tom's parents shared a similar dis-ease. Frozen out by parents and siblings, they got on with life, bearing children and moving to Scotland. Tom trained as a church minister, and today serves a parish. Eventually, ten years after their wedding, respective parents are a little more understanding, and for the first time, Tom's parents have spent a holiday with them.

Here's a different mixed marriage:

Paulo is Italian and lives with his wife and two children in the Cumbria countryside. A quiet family man, Paulo has his own desk top publishing business, earning a modest annual income. The children are schooled locally and his wife, Beth, is a nurse. Respected, well adjusted, the model of a decent family. Except that Paulo used to be a Catholic priest. In his own mind, he is still a priest. In marrying Beth he provoked the disapprobation of the Vatican, resulting in a **rapid and brutal exit from the priesthood.** According to Paulo he feels more complete as a man and has a lot more to offer in terms of ministry. He feels betrayed, abandoned and deeply misunderstood.

Jesus went out of his way to welcome and befriend foreigners, strangers, and the marginalised. For example, he

▪ strikes up a conversation with Samaritan woman of dubious reputation;

- tells a story of a Samaritan who is good and generous;

- says that Sodom and Gommorah will fare better than Jewish cities on the day of judgement;

- gives words of hope to a dying criminal;

- refuses to condemn a woman caught in adultery.

The Messiah's example was repeated in the earliest days of the church:

- Peter dreams of a meat feast that breaks all the Jewish food laws.

- Cornelius, a Roman, receives Christ and is filled with the Spirit.

- Paul, a Jewish theologian, develops a love for gentiles.

- Christians are first given that name in the multi-racial church of Antioch.

- Rome replaces Jerusalem as the capital of the church.

Ruth's radical commitment to Naomi and her God is an inspiration today. She walked a long way to realise her destiny, and Jesus is still bringing many like her to glory.

Remember...

In bringing many sons [and daughters] to glory, it was fitting that God, for whom and through whom everything exists, should make the author of their salvation perfect through suffering. Hebrews 2:10

Ruth, the outsider, becomes a member, through Jesus.

God sets the lonely in families... **Psalm 68:6**

If that's true of some of our own families, then it's so much more true of God's family. In God's family there are

no ghettos

no cliques

no special members' bars

no private chat rooms

no privileged classes

That's the theory, at any rate. Sadly, we, you, they get it wrong much of the time and make the church seem like an exclusive club. But keep your eyes on Jesus and all the Ruths that surround him. He's gone to extreme lengths to make as many friends as possible from as far away as possible:

Therefore, remember that formerly you who are Gentiles by birth and called 'uncircumcised' by those who call themselves 'the circumcision' (that done in the body by the hands of men) — remember that at that time you were separate from Christ, excluded from citizenship in Israel and foreigners to the covenants of the promise, without hope and without God in the world. But now in Christ Jesus you who once were far away have been brought near through the blood of Christ.

For he himself is our peace, who has made the two one and has destroyed the barrier, the dividing wall of hostility, by abolishing in his flesh the law with its commandments and regulations. His purpose was to create in himself one new man [person] out of the two, thus making peace, and in this one body to reconcile both of them to God through the cross, by which he put to death their hostility. He came and preached peace to you who were far away and peace to those who were near. For through him we have access to the Father by one Spirit. Ephesians 2:11-18

And maybe another mixed marriage in the making is this one:

Kishan is a young Asian man. Part of a close family, he is steeped in Islam and his culture's impressive attitudes towards family and social life. He has few Christian friends, but during Year 12 at secondary school he meets Judith, an attractive white student. They share the same English class. Friendship develops and they begin to date each other. Before long they realise that the differences between them are serious and it becomes a matter for concern. Individually, they relate well. But they bring to each other **the echoes and whispers of centuries.** She: white, middle-class, prosperous, Christian. He: black, Muslim, working class, new money. Both have kept their friendship a secret from their families.

One Sunday evening, Kishan accompanies Judith to her church. Expecting a tower, spire, robes, smells, white faces, he is surprised. They visit a school hall, full of people, variety of races, led by a woman. The music is transatlantic, not unpleasant. Someone speaks on the parable of the Prodigal Son. A very simple sentence stands out for him: 'God is looking to forgive you.' This haunts him for the next week. God as judge, holy, forbidding, perfect, mighty. Fine. But **God as forgiver?** God as forgiver who loves simply because that's his nature?

Kishan is puzzled, captivated, frightened. It's a God he doesn't know but he can't dismiss it as white, Western, culture specific. He wants to know God. Not just Judith's God, but the God who is looking to forgive him, and everyone else.

He loves Judith and feels that maybe it's time to make God his home.

Chapter 6: my wife next door

chapter 6
my wife next door

David was the father of Solomon, whose mother had been Uriah's wife. <u>Matthew 1:6</u>

I know someone who had an influential meeting.

'Small towns often hide big secrets. Once, as a young twenty-something, I met **the most powerful judge in England.** His career had been long, littered with dazzling judgements and very controversial. Before introducing him, I ought to explain how this meeting came about.

'Thursday afternoon, early autumn, 1982. I was studying, haphazardly and terminally, to be a barrister. Based in London's ancient Middle Temple, I soon learnt a new definition of being called to the bar. I had access to the cheapest saloon in London, and the cost of a double G and T was laughably low.

'The morning after a particularly heavy night, I received a strange invitation. Someone I vaguely knew asked me to attend the Lawyers' Christian Fellowship that afternoon. For a reason I cannot remember, I accepted. I was **a lapsed and deeply frozen Christian**, and gave eager Christians a very wide berth. I was no Sleeping Beauty but I was in need of a reviving encounter with the Prince of Peace. Except that I studiously avoided any brush with the divine.

'I turned up at an address in nearby Lincoln's Inn Fields, clad in an threadbare Aran jumper, holey jeans and something of a headache. My first mistake. Most of the people, including the students, were suited. Even worse, I'd slept in my clothes the night before. More of a night on the carpet than the tiles. In Cricklewood, as I recall. Next to leaving, my first instinct was to drink the bone china cup of tea that was offered me. It was then I noticed the urn. Never seen such an elaborate piece of tannin architecture in my life. Not only was the lid adorned with hand-crafted silver elephants, but the tap was shaped in the form of the aforementioned animal's trunk. All silver. We huddled together, making awkward conversation. Actually, it was probably me doing the awkward huddling.

'Sipping my tea, surrounded by the quiet murmurs of sanctified advocates, I became aware of another's presence. An elderly white haired man was making his way around the group, introducing himself and engaging in small talk. I'd seen him somewhere before but couldn't place his face. As he made his way I suddenly recognised him and itched to leave at once. Too late — he was in front of me. "Hello I'm Lord Denning, I've come to talk to you all today. What's your name?" **S h a m e** is not the word. Not only did he enjoy a massive reputation in the legal and political fraternity, but he'd journeyed direct from the law courts. The works. Gown, tabs, buckled shoes, garters. Thank God he wasn't sporting a wig. And there I stood, a dirty pullover soiled with last night's lager and curry. But he was very sweet and he moved on to the people next to me. Eventually he addressed us all. Spoke of the novels of Sir Walter Scott, the writings of Disraeli, and `the impact of the Bible` on his life. It wasn't so much what he said as the way he said it. Here was a man who commanded the attention of Britain's most powerful figures and yet his accent was as moist and rural as his native Hampshire. Son of a village cobbler, he had retained his identity and gloried in being different. He both amused and alarmed the Establishment because he sounded like the men who drove their cars or fed their sheep. He lived in the village in which he was born.'

Yes, small towns yield epic characters:

- William Carey, pioneer of missionary work in India, started out as a cobbler in a Northamptonshire village.

- Abraham Lincoln, often regarded as America's greatest president, was born in a log cabin in Kentucky.

- Oscar winning actor Anthony Hopkins grew up in the South Wales town of Port Talbot.

Bethlehem is hardly the home of radical chic. Today it sits uncomfortably between Palestinian and Israeli tensions. It's **an urban timebomb**. Travel back about three thousand years ago and what would you find? It's there: a place of modest dwellings, a few tents, dirt tracks and sheep. Lots of sheep. This is hill country, rich grazing land in the south of Judea. Bethlehem is one of the Old Testament's oldest towns, mentioned in the story of Jacob, but its original name is even more ancient: Ephrath (Genesis 35:16). This was a place for rednecks, hill-billies and sheep rustlers. Shepherds. Picture the humble rustic youth, reclining against a fruitful olive tree, playing his pan pipes. Chewing grapes, he dozes in the warm afternoon, occasionally glancing at his plump sheep. Right? Baloney! It was a hard, and often dangerous occupation. Shepherds were:

- often at the bottom of the career pile;

- exposed to the extremes of heat and cold;

- forced to eat meagre amounts of food found in the wild;

- at the mercy of lions, wolves, panthers and bears;

- lonely — enduring days, sometimes weeks, on their own.

Bethlehem was also **a king cradle**. The greatest king ever seen in Israel came from a shepherding background. His father, Jesse, grandson of Boaz, enjoyed no social importance. Like virtually every other man in the area, his livelihood depended on the vagaries of the world's most stupid and loveable creatures. Having several sons, none were destined for greatness. Until the day of the prophet. Samuel arrived, commanded by God to find the next King of Israel. Led to Jesse's family, he asks to inspect each of the sons, expecting to recognise God's anointed. Six faces pass before him and none of them impress. He enquires if there is another. Yes, and he's out in the fields tending the sheep. Of course. David is ushered in, oil is poured, and powerful words of coronation are proclaimed. A teenager whose hands and feet are covered in sheep dung is the **chosen of God**.

One problem. Israel already had a king. A mad, sad, musical, jealous and demonised inadequate. Saul. But it's all sorted out in a typical Old Testament swashbuckling and buccaneering sort of way. Success, humanity, prosperity and massive ratings in the opinion polls now followed him. Surrounded by fawning courtiers, his aroma was perfumed, exotic even. You couldn't smell the fields now. Moreover he was bored. Bizarrely, every so often eastern kings timetabled battles and skirmishes against each other. It happened regularly. On one such occasion, David stayed at home, while his men and all the neighbouring despots gathered to knock each other about. Not David. David was bored. Bored, middle-aged men sometimes engage in stupid and disastrous acts. Just like David. Away from the company of his peers and rivals, he indulged his weakness. Spying his neighbour's voluptuous wife, he eyed an opportunity for seduction. She was beautiful and she was available. This is what happened:

- he abused his power and they had sex (probably lots of sex);

A teenager whose hands and feet are covered in sheep dung is the chosen of God.

- she became pregnant;

- he called Uriah, her husband, home from the war, hoping that husband and wife would have sex (this would clear David, seeming as though the child was Uriah's);

- Uriah refused to sleep with her;

- David sent him back, arranging for him to be killed in battle;

- David married Bathsheeba;

- the child died — as a result of God's punishment on David.

One Old Testament scholar has suggested a twist to the story. He claims that Uriah knew all along that his wife was pregnant by another man. His research indicates that a soldier at this period could only return from battle if —

a) his next of kin had died, or

b) his wife was pregnant.

Bathsheba wasn't dead, so she must be pregnant. And there could only be one father. The moment Uriah returned home he was caught up in gross political and emotional manipulation. Refusing to lie with his wife would yield only one outcome. His death. Uriah became a fatal distraction.

But what of Bathsheba? She doesn't even get mentioned by name in Matthew's tree. Known simply as so-and-so's wife. Demeaning. Happens a lot in families. Think of all the times you have been referred to as so-and-so's

wife

husband

son

daughter

Matthew is so embarrassed by this story that he blushes at her name. Apparently this was not unknown in the literary circles of his day. Adulterous women were worthy only of being forgotten. But Matthew can't do that, because she's a vital part of Jesus' story. Without her, he wouldn't have been the Saviour he became. I love that. Matthew can't ignore her, neither can we, and God has already welcomed her into the family of faith. Sadly, she is remembered as a

scarlet woman

slag

scrubber

good time girl

slut

Just some of the words — the names — used to describe her actions. Adultery always produces ambivalence in other people. An unfaithful man is regarded as a cheat and scoundrel, but he's only pursuing his hormonal destiny. The woman, however, enjoys no such status. She's manipulative, conniving, a breaker of homes.

Joy, 56, lives with her partner Jeremy. Both have been previously married, but have now been together for six years. Since she left her husband 20 years ago, Joy has had several affairs and relationships, some of which have lasted for a number of years. She has three children, and the moment she left their father was the last time she saw them. She has virtually been **disowned** by her own family.

The innocent human product of the David and Bathsheba liaison died. Despite David's repentance, God allowed the child to pass away before sampling life. Terrifying. Sin has consequences, sometimes apparently unjustly so. A baby has no moral or legal responsibility, but his father's callous folly causes his own demise.

David's adultery marked the end of his golden era. Read his story and discover that his political achievements, military success, spiritual authority were all expressed before his affair with Bathsheba. He

> united a torn kingdom
>
> established peace
>
> extended his nation's boundaries
>
> passed humane laws
>
> restored worship to the centre of Jerusalem...

...all prior to his extra-marital affair. Adultery **diminished** David. Reduced him. He lived to witness the precocious and incompetent bunglings of his successor Solomon. Even worse was his grief over the death of Absalom, one of his other sons. Absalom rebelled against his father's rule and established himself as an anti-king, an alternative ruler. Mustered an army of malcontents and stormed Jerusalem, intent on seizing power. Despite this treachery, David yearned for a restored relationship with his son. He died suddenly and brutally. When riding through a thicket his head was caught in branches whilst his horse careered on. Death by hanging. David's lament was raw, distressing and deeply authentic. On hearing the news we read:

> The king was shaken. He went up to the room over the gateway and wept. As he went, he said: 'O my son Absalom! My son, my son Absalom! If only I had died instead of you – O Absalom, my son, my son!' 2 Samuel 18:33

Adultery always has **consequences.** And generally these go beyond those directly involved. Take Stephen, for example. Stephen is in his mid-forties and, should you meet him today, you would observe a married man with a toddler tugging at his trouserlegs. Calm, affluent, desirable lifestyle. On the face of it. Rewind four years. Stephen is married to Karen, a partnership that has lasted for 23 years. Along with their two daughters, Stephen and Karen have moved several times within the UK, living in various towns and cities. This itinerant lifestyle is not purely a matter of chasing better jobs and bigger incomes. They are both deeply involved in a new church network, eager to serve God's purposes. As a trained accountant, Stephen understands money and how it is made. He has financial green fingers, at least when it comes to business and other people's money. His own monetary affairs are at best precarious. Moving to a large city, he persuades a venture capital company to invest in his new enterprise: wholesaling and distributing organic fruit and vegetables. Successful marketing yields fantastic results and within a few months he has persuaded several large supermarket chains to sell his product. In tandem with business joy, Stephen and Karen immerse themselves in a new church plant in the city. Karen pursues an inner healing and counselling ministry, whilst Stephen helps the church's embryonic leadership think strategically, especially in terms of mission and spiritual warfare.

But the background scenery is **collapsing**. Mr and Mrs Zealous Christian have chronic marriage difficulties, partially eclipsed through years of travel, business and non-communication. She feels unloved and unappreciated. He feels bored. This is the feeling he most identifies with. Boredom. Bored with his marriage, with his work and with his faith. Despite his confident and self-assured exterior, he struggles with massive intimations of failure and low self-esteem. His manhood is **crying out** for compensation and colour.

Skeletons and consequences: Stephen's adultery.

Something to add fizz, colour, change. Something for the weekend. Powerful, uncomfortable, delicious yearnings, way beyond the reach of his withering theology. He can pray a good prayer in public, but his inner life is drawn to **forbidden fruit.**

Stephen and Karen don't make love any more. Hardly speak. But as a family, they look good in church. The girls are popular and their parents are faking the life of faith, and doing it successfully. Until. Stephen decides he needs to beef up his company's profile and appoints a PR officer. Out of the several applicants he chooses a young, single, attractive woman. Jennifer. Yes, it's inevitable. Starts with mild flirtation, long evenings spent in the office. Then there's a business trip to Brussels. That's where it happens. Late at night in the hotel bar, after several drinks, they cuddle on the leather sofa opposite the log fire. Night of fumbled passion. Home the next day. Stephen has now hurled a bomb into his private world. Spends the remainder of the week in long hours and early mornings.

Karen senses something is deeply wrong and she tells him so. He denies it initially, then comes the admission and her wounded rage. He leaves her and the two bewildered teenagers, moving into a nearby hotel. Church gets involved, pleading for reconciliation, restoration, repentance. He's not interested. The journey down the slippery slope has proved considerably faster than he'd imagined. What's going on? Surrounded by a devastated family life, broken promises, **betrayal**, shell-shot daughters, how does he feel about it all? No regrets. Should never have got married in the first place; people said we shouldn't have. Twenty-three years ago. His daughters don't share this retro opinion and his wife feels serrated by Stephen's actions.

He eventually moves in with Jennifer, jettisoning friendships, family ties, nursing his own pain.

Torn marriage, broken children, incredulous Christian community. But there's other afterglow to this piece of life-threatening radiation. His business collapses. Spectacularly. Supermarkets withdraw his products on the basis that they no longer match their criteria. Staff are made redundant, receivers are called in, he's declared bankrupt. Humiliated entrepreneur — and then Jennifer discovers she is pregnant.

Another move, another city, another home, another job. Another marriage.

And on the face of it he's doing very nicely. Thank you. **Skin-deep contentment** when you consider the legal wranglings with his ex-, anorexic illness of his younger daughter and apparent strains in this new marriage. He has a son, but what sort of inheritance is this?

People commit adultery when

- they can longer bear the loneliness of their marriage;

- they dislike their own company;

- major life change produces severe emotional disorientation;

- boredom has seeped into everything.

Successful relationships rely on **trust**. Faithfulness. Probably the most neglected and overlooked of qualities. Compared to

flare

creativity

risk

achievement

self-fulfilment...

faithfulness seems tame, grey, undesirable. But it's the foundation of everything. It provides the **oxygen** for any healthy relationship. Only in its absence is it truly appreciated. Without it — chaos, suspicion, breakdown. **I know someone**, a pastor, who regularly speaks these words to the men in his congregation: 'Rehearse the consequences of your adultery.'

Yes, think how suicidal it will make your wife feel. Imagine the betrayal experienced by your children. Consider the shattering disbelief forced upon your colleagues, neighbours, church. Adultery models unfaithfulness as a way of life. Presents itself as an alternative.

But there can't be anyone who hasn't been tempted. Some have escaped from the jaws of their failure. A young married church elder got involved with a woman in his church. Counselling led to emotional bonding and near-fatal attraction. Comically, undressed and in bed with each other, engaging in foreplay, he realises what he's doing. He **sees** it. Grabbing his clothes, mumbling apologies, he runs out of the house and into the street. Even though it is 2am he hurries to his pastor's house, chimes the bell until lights appear and a familiar face peers through the frosted glass. Rushes in, mixture of tears, mild hysteria and disjointed sentences. Confesses all. The pastor listens and then they both return to the young man's home and visit his wife, who is sick with worry at her husband's unannounced absence. Eventually his marriage is saved, as is his calling. But it takes time. This is a happy story. There are many others which conclude in ruin, bitterness, and waste.

Curiously, David receives a good press in the New Testament. Jesus is compared to him and is born in his city. In the Gospels Jesus is referred to as a son of David and during his triumphal entry in Jerusalem on Palm Sunday, he is acclaimed as a son of this discredited king. The family link is applauded.

Why? Many possible answers but I'm going with two of them.

Firstly, David's kingship was **a blessing to the nation**. Through his mixture of spirituality, political authority and concern for the underprivileged, he made royalty work.

And secondly, **he was a heart man.** Saul, whose reign came to a savage and depressing end, had been a head and shoulders man. That was the basis of his appointment. He was head and shoulders over his contemporaries. Physically imposing, he could talk a good fight. In reality he was massively insecure, jealous and indecisive. David, on the other hand, knew God and he knew himself. Before he ruled the nation he had learnt intimacy with God. In his flight from Saul and in his fight with his enemies he mastered the art of inquiring of God. When finally uniting the kingdom and making Jerusalem its capital, he realises that her true king is God. Rescuing the ark of the covenant from Obed Edom's backyard, he marshals this throne of grace to Mount Zion. His entry into Jerusalem is marked by a frenzied, ecstatic, naked dance, prompting pure scorn from his wife, Michal:

> 'How the king of Israel has distinguished himself today, disrobing in the sight of the slave girls of his servants as any vulgar fellow would.' **2 Samuel 6:20**

David's response is immediate and unashamed, displaying his reckless abandonment in God:

> 'It was before the Lord, who chose me rather than your father or anyone from his house when he appointed me ruler over the Lord's people Israel — I will celebrate before the Lord. I will become even more undignified than this, and I will be humiliated in my own eyes. But by these slave girls you spoke of, I will be held in honour.' **2 Samuel 6:21,22**

But, to return to David's weakness. Adultery wreaks havoc on everyone within range. But God sees **beyond** it. Maybe you can't. Could it be that you have been betrayed by one who owned your heart? Maybe you discovered that your husband was having an affair with a mutual friend. You feel you'll never recover from this pain. Or is it you who has been unfaithful? And now you are in bitter regret.

Jesus was proud to be associated with the name of David; happy to be identified with colossal strength and titanic failure. Jesus took David to the cross with him, travailing through every nightmare:

betrayal

murder

deception

cot death

Jesus also is bringing many Davids with him into glory. Broken kings, discredited heroes, wounded bravehearts. Those who turn towards him in faith, walking away from deceitful relationships, will be privy to this exchange with the risen Christ.

'Martin, John, Peter, Jane, Trisha, Helen... where are they? Has no one condemned you?'

Say it.

'No one, sir.'

'Then neither do I condemn you,' Jesus declared. 'Go now and leave your life of sin.' John 8:11

As you live in the good of Jesus' love for you, you are

free from accusation

free from condemnation

empowered to live a new life

part of his family

Welcome.

Chapter 7:teenage virgin conceives

Mary is an exceptional girl. Stretch your imagination and you won't find a more remarkable teenager. Observe her life from any angle, viewpoint, perspective and you'll reach the same conclusion. You see, there's something about Mary. She's in Year 10 preparing for next year's GCSEs. Diligent, hard-working, conscientious. But that's not the point. Yes, at times dazzlingly creative, even had some of her poems published. Not of the essence. Listen to what her teacher said in last year's report: 'A good year for Mary, demonstrating excellent work and attitude. I must say that it's a delight having her at this school. Mary possesses great moral purpose, she has a vision of how society should be ordered, some might call it **a spiritual vision**'.

Spiritual vision. Can't you see it?

...He has performed mighty deeds with his arm; he has scattered those who are proud in their inmost thoughts. He has brought down rulers from their thrones but has lifted up the humble. He has filled the hungry with good things but has sent the rich away empty...
From Mary's song, Luke 1:51-53

Quiet, unassuming, but sometimes terrifyingly intense. Dreamy, lateral, and yet she brings clarity to any conversation. In the same report, Year 10's RE teacher gave the following observation: 'Mary satisfactorily completed her modules on the Trinity, the supernatural in religion and the problem of pain. Her extended essay on the history of angels in Judaism was outstanding.'

There's something about Mary. On the face of it she's an ordinary fourteen-year-old. Many friends, but not outstandingly popular, close-knit family, and religious. To a point. Maybe that's what so `singular` about her. She's very committed to her church, both in attendance and in contribution, but (and this is hard to explain), she's not defined by it. This is probably what her teacher sensed, an indefinable and sometimes strange quality. Years later, some of her friends remarked that it was as though Mary had a relationship with God. Many could write about him, argue the toss one way or the other, but above all it was as though she knew him. But all this was said some years after *the* event. As far as now is concerned, her reputation has suffered a dramatic blow.

'I have no pleasure in writing to you about this,' began a recent letter from the headmaster to Mary's parents, 'but this is a religious school, and both governors and parents alike have certain `expectations`, especially concerning the practice of morality within the school.'

As may be observed, all is not well. He continues: 'We are bitterly disappointed at Mary's conduct. Not only is her pregnancy a source of considerable dismay — she was an exemplary student — but her current attitude is highly regrettable. Her student counsellor, Mrs Jeavons, has spoken to her several times, but has found Mary very uncooperative. As far as I can ascertain, Mary displays no remorse for her actions and I am left with no choice, other than to ask you to meet with me, Mary's head of year, and of course, Mary. Here are a few possible dates.'

This summons comes as a complete surprise to Mary's parents. Bizarre as it may seem, they have no idea. Only a couple of months gone and no physical signs. No swelling of the abdomen, no morning sickness, no strange dietary habits. Normal.

`...it was as though Mary had a relationship with God.`

This is how the headmaster came to know. Shortly after some weird events in Mary's life, she confided in a friend, actually a cousin, who also attended St Gabriel's. So surprised and horrified was Lizzie by the news that she told several other people, one of whom harboured a secret loathing for Mary. Detested her God-talk and so-called spirituality. Seeing an opportunity for character ruination, she beat a crooked path to the headmaster's door and gave him the entire story. With a few **embellishments**, just to make it a little more spicy. Incredulous headmaster sent for Mary, causing her to leave a Geography lesson.

He asks several leading questions and ascertains that she is indeed pregnant and, yes, she knows the father. Her straightforward admission stuns him. Unbeknown to Mary, a number of senior staff and governors have already suggested her as a future head girl, a foolish and dangerous whim in the light of this news. He simply doesn't know what to say and when finally he manages to say something it ends in a strangulated cough. Even when at ease with the world and himself he is a tense man, but over the next half an hour he shatters his own personal record for provoked anger.

Mary sits silently, watching her headmaster build up a head of poisonous steam. Unlike many others, his rage manifests itself in the form of quiet, deliberate and yet menacing sentences. The combination of deep baritone, pronounced Wiltshire burr and carefully cadenced sentences portrays him both as thug and clown at the same time. He begins. 'You have deceived us. You have sat with your colleagues over these years in various and sundry lessons, and you have deceived us. You have enjoyed a transparent reputation amongst us all, gaining the favour of the teaching staff and you have chosen to repay us in a deeply offensive manner.'

Mary says nothing, quietly observing the small sponge of foam forming at the right corner of his mouth.

'I cannot tell you how shocked I am and adequately convey the sense of being personally let down. Furthermore, this bitter disappointment is shared by many others.' With this he flourishs before her a sheet of A4, through which she sees a series of typed paragraphs.

'These are from some of our leading governors who have heard the news.' Reeling off a series of **astonishments, disappointments, ejaculations and exclamations**, Mary begins to feel the weight of condemnation. From the peak of faxed outrage, the Rev Dr John Zacharias moderates his quivering tremolo, leans towards her, his corpulent torso resting on podgy arms and says: 'Mary, this is an ancient school. This is a religious school. We are proud of our traditions and guard them zealously. We had thought that you, too, viewed yourself as a trustee of this **godly inheritance**.' He pauses, savouring the beauty of the sentence. Continuing with a question, he now indicates that it is time for Mary to respond: 'How on earth has this happened? Why did you allow such a terrible compromise and sin to enter your life? Mary, I need an answer.'

Up to this point, Mary has said nothing, made no response, body language has remained non-committal, aloof. She hears the opprobrium, implied threats, force of collective anger. But none of it invades her mind. She is a curious young woman. From an early age, her life has been noticed, commented upon. Family, friends, school teachers, church, regularly voice their admiration of her 'qualities'. These are never precisely defined but acknowledge an inner calm, a commitment to holy and just relationships and a mystical view of everything that surrounds her. But she is never a conformist. Others see her as different and this is how she views herself.

Sitting opposite her morally fuming superior, she has no appetite for justification. However a question has been posted and an answer must be mailed.

'Dr Zacharias, you will struggle to believe my reply and you may find it offensive. My pregnancy is a source of **astonishment** to me, but not shame. I have nothing for which to repent or apologise. God did this to me.'

'He's doing a new thing on this planet...'

Dr Zacharias is about to hurl a few word grenades at her, but Mary raises her hands, signalling her desire to continue, uninterrupted.

'Three months ago I received a visit. It was late, Mum and Dad had gone to bed and I had finished a piece of course work. I was watching the television, *Newsnight* I think, when I noticed that I was not alone. Sitting across from me, in the armchair next to the sound system, was a young man about my age. He was dressed in jeans and a Fatboy Slim tee-shirt.'

This cultural reference is wasted on the Rev Dr.

'I was so shocked that I spilt my hot chocolate. I was really scared. His dress was familiar but everything else was frightening. Who was he, how had he got in and what was he going to do with me? He was black, muscular and couldn't stop smiling. He could see that I was scared rigid, so he began talking to me. "Hi sister, I've got some wonderful news for you. I've come from God and he thinks that you are really special. He's noticed you and he likes your attitude, the way you go about your life. I've come to tell you some important news that will affect you and actually the world. You see, you're pregnant."

'Despite my alarm, I manage a "No, I'm not. I'm a virgin. I've never slept with anyone."

'"Sister hear me out, let me finish. You are pregnant with God's baby. He's doing **a new thing on this planet** and you are now part of this great new plan. It's hard to explain but he's sending himself, coming as a baby. But that's not the point, at least not for you at the moment. The thing is, you will be the way he enters the world. He wants to become as much a human being as anyone else and he realises that he needs to be formed in your womb, born and be totally vulnerable. <u>So Father God has decided that Son God will be born in you and Holy Spirit God has already done it.</u> He has planted a unique egg in your womb and in nine months' time you will give birth to a son who will bring liberty to the whole earth.'"

Mary falls silent again.

Dr Zacharias can contain himself no longer. 'How dare you speak like this. Get out this instant, you wicked child! This is blasphemy of the worst kind. God would never do such thing and he'd never use you. You're just a child — and an evil one at that.'

Mary was expelled. She didn't get a school report this year.

Such a familiar, unfamilar story. Familiar. **Of the family.** Narrated each Christmas to the anthem of well-loved carols, smell of mince pies and cheery TV programmes. All well and good, but in the last resort, and even the first, it's a scandal. Old Testament law prescribes corporal punishment on virgins who are found to be sexually active. For example:

> If a man happens to meet in a town a virgin pledged to be married and he sleeps with her, you shall take both of them to the gate of that town and stone them to death — the girl because she was in a town and did not scream for help, and the man because he violated another man's wife. You must purge the evil from among you. <u>Deuteronomy 22:23,24</u>

Granted, Mary's story is not that of a promiscuous teenager, but it does involve God mysteriously impregnating a virgin. This could lead to some misunderstanding. What is God doing, making a young woman vulnerable to death at the hands of her religious masters? God was

▪ presenting **a new start** to the world.
Through a young woman of exceptional faith and
sexual innocence, Jesus was birthed. It's
interesting that the phrase 'Mary, the mother of
God' wasn't coined in order to venerate Mary but
to honour the fact that the child in her womb
was none other than God.

▪ presenting **a radical critique** of family
life. From now on, pedigree, background,
genealogy, mean nothing. The family of faith is
always first generation. No blue blood, royal lines
or privilege. Not even grandparents or parents in
any conventional sense. Paul the apostle refers to
the need for fathers in God, but this refers to the
need for powerful role models in the church, even
as Paul was:

Even though you have ten thousand guardians
in Christ, you do not have many fathers, for in
Christ Jesus I became your father through the
gospel. **1 Corinthians 4:15**

> He takes the
> wretched stuff
> of our minds
> and lives and
> transforms them
> into something
> wonderfully
> beautiful.

As we have followed the life and times of Matthew's women
and the many other people mentioned in this book, one
overwhelming issue seems to stand out. It's this: <u>What matters
most is not where this person comes from, but what God is
doing in their lives now. And how they are responding to his
call.</u> These women remind us that God's dealings with us are
often surprising, sometimes breathtaking, and always
gracious. He takes the wretched stuff of our minds and lives
and transforms them into something wonderfully beautiful. At
any time, you might have been attempted to abort the process.
Too much mess, rottenness, depravity. But there are **no
abortions** in God's economy. Each apparent disaster merely
prepares more underlay for God's red carpet. He's preparing

for the entry of the Son he loves, whose journey will be through the genes and jams of his predecessors.

This tells me that:

- there are no mistakes with God;

- he is able to rescue the most dismal situation;

- faith in Jesus means a creative partnership with the God of heaven;

- God cannot be shocked by human failure;

- wounded people have the most interesting stories;

- the Christian family is not another version of the nuclear variety.

Here's an example of what God has done in the history of one family, told in the words of Terry:

'We don't have skeletons in our cupboard — we have the whole damn cemetery. My parents' marriage became ugly in the late 70s. They were separated for 11 years. This was at a time when separation and divorce were not really in vogue, so I guess they were trendsetters in a sense.

'My mum became a Christian, then a few years later my dad became a Christian. Now, my dad is one of those people who — all of us know the type — would never come to Christ. Except he did. My parents changed. They re-affirmed their wedding vows. They are truly married again and have been going strong ever since.

'I value that God has restored my parents' marriage, healed unbelievable hurt and forgiven much. I have learned incredible lessons from my parents about unconditional love, acceptance, forgiveness, grace, hope, long-suffering and faith in our Lord Jesus Christ.

'Strangely, even though I would not want to ever experience certain segments of my childhood again, and I would want no one else to go through these things, I am not sure I would change anything. **God's hand** was in it all, even though we may not have recognised it all the time.

'Even my parent's non-Christian friends thank God and are amazed at the transformation!'

This is Terry's mother's additional comment:

'I have prayed for marriages knowing that the Lord wanted to heal and restore them, but the Christian partner just wanted to get on with life and they divorced. To **hang in there** invites a lot of abuse from Christian and non-Christian armchair psychologists who cannot see that the Lord takes his time to work in the heart of the "waiting" person. It is very hard to trust in the Lord's promise, yet to have the "world" pull you down and mock you every day especially during the "it gets worse before it gets better" times. But the result is priceless and becomes the envy of all the mockers. Praise the Lord — for his lovingkindness endures forever.'

How do we leave Matthew's five women? And what about all the others, some of whom are alive, others dead? And what about my great grandmother, known only to me by way of a fragment, a shared collective memory? This is what:

After this I looked and there before me was a great multitude that no-one could count, from every nation, tribe, people and language, standing before the throne and in front of the Lamb. They were wearing white robes and were holding palm branches in their hands. And they cried out in a loud voice:

'Salvation belongs to our God, who sits on the throne, and to the Lamb.'

A few lines later and we read this:

Then one of the elders asked me, 'These in white robes — who are they, and where did they come from?'

I answered, 'Sir, you know.'

And he said, 'These are they who have come out of the great tribulation; they have washed their robes and made them white in the blood of the Lamb. Therefore,

'they are before the throne of God
    and serve him day and night in his temple;
and he who sits on the throne will spread his tent over them.
Never again will they hunger;
    never again will they thirst.
The sun will not beat upon them,
    nor any scorching heat.
For the lamb at the centre of the throne will be their shepherd;
    he will lead them to springs of living water.
And God will wipe away every tear from their eyes.'
<u>Revelation 7: 9,10, 13-17</u>

Look closely at this vast crowd. No look again, don't be phased by the numbers. Scan the faces, the various colours. Recognise anyone? No. Search, zoom, focus. It's getting clearer. In the midst of the great and the good there are plenty of surprises. You mean, he got in? Then there's that row of women. Five of them. Look, really look. Tamar, Rahab, Ruth, Bathsheeba, Mary. No longer wearing the frowns of hard living, or sporting emotional scars, but laughing, radiant, dancing. They've been transformed by Jesus, and the soil of past trauma and sin has been washed away. Over there, with some other people, that's my great-grandmother. This is an even bigger praise meeting than the one she saw in 1859. But before you return to your life, take another peep. There's someone else you recognise in this cathedral of worship. Someone at peace, happy, loving it, singing with lungs that will never burst. A person whose life is now swallowed up in Christ's cosmic glory, hidden in him, gazing at the sheer joy of eternal life.

It's you.